Watch out for deceptive voices—worldly voices making

promises, Christian voices calling for commitments that

don't fit into Christ's will and ways. Beware of enemies

with smiling faces.

COLOSSIANS 2:8 (PARAPHRASED)

Enemies with Smiling Faces

DEFEATING

THE SUBTLE

THREATS THAT

ENDANGER

CHRISTIANS

Donald C. Posterski

InterVarsity Press
Downers Grove, Illinois

InterVarsity Press
P.O. Box 1400, Downers Grove, IL 60515-1426
World Wide Web: www.ivpress.com
E-mail: mail@ivpress.com

InterVarsity Press® is the book-publishing division of InterVarsity Christian Fellowship/USA®, a student movement active on campus at hundreds of universities, colleges and schools of nursing in the United States of America, and a member movement of the International Fellowship of Evangelical Students. For information about local and regional activities, write Public Relations Dept., InterVarsity Christian Fellowship/USA, 6400 Schroeder Rd., P.O. Box 7895, Madison, WI 53707-7895, or visit the IVCF website at <www.ivcf.org>.

Scripture is taken from the New Revised Standard Version of the Bible, copyright 1989 by the Division of Christian Education of the National Council of the Churches of Christ in the USA. Used by permission.

Cover design: Cindy Kiple

Cover images: snake: Digital Vision
                 happy face: Photodisc Blue/Getty Images

ISBN 0-8308-2387-5

Printed in the United States of America ∞

Library of Congress Cataloging-in-Publication Data

Posterski, Donald C., 1942-
    Enemies with smiling faces: defeating the subtle threats that
endanger Christians /Donald C. Posterski.
        p. cm.
Includes bibliographical references.
    ISBN 0-8308-2387-5 (pbk.: alk. paper)
    1. Christian life. I. Title.
    BV4501.3.P67 2004
    248.4—dc22

                                                                    2003025922

P	18	17	16	15	14	13	12	11	10	9	8	7	6	5	4	3	2	1
Y	17	16	15	14	13	12	11	10	09	08	07	06	05	04				

Timothy Foley . . .

pastor

priest

friend

encourager

Contents

Introduction

As we talked on the phone, I could feel the emotional weight my friend was carrying. Then came the lament of his soul: "Life is a pretty disappointing affair."

Two tragic episodes had scarred my friend. In both instances, Christian people who on the surface deserved to be trusted had deceived and betrayed him. And though his faith and health are strong, and though he is vocationally competent and professionally successful, for Craig life is a crushing disappointment.

"So what's the big deal?" some people will say. "Welcome to life. It sounds like Craig is better off than most of us. Life hurts some of the time. Tell him to stop moping and move on."

Craig *will* move on. He's strong enough to regroup and try again. But next time he will be more careful. He's been damaged. He will be reticent in forming relational commitments. He'll no longer be so ready to trust in the apparent integrity of others. The painful memories will never be completely erased.

Life is not what Craig expected it would be. The love of his life and a cherished friend had turned on him. Intimacy and trust and laughter and expectation collapsed on top of him. The same people who had given him the best moments of life now were inflicting deep torment.

They became his enemies with smiling faces.

All of us have been hurt by others. If we are honest with ourselves, we know we have also hurt others. Sometimes our words have been intended to cause harm. Other times, without our awareness, our actions have wounded people and afflicted them with sleepless nights.

Our experience with pain is not limited to human relationships. We are also familiar with spiritual pain. While we may have difficulty admitting it out loud, there have been times when we were disappointed with God. Most of us are careful not to blame God directly. Instead we harp on the shortcomings of the church, the inadequacies of the minister or the hypocrisy of Christians who claim more than they live. That is how some of us tend to express our disappointment with God. Others who are more self-blaming reason, "My disappointments reflect my spiritual incompleteness."

Since I have known Luke, he has always been serious about his faith. In fact it is hard to think of him without immediately thinking of the Christ he knows and loves. That's why I was so surprised at a recent casual meal we had together. Having just handed our menus back to our server, he blurted out, "Frankly, Don, I'm tired of covering up for God."

Believing that friendship includes uncensored acceptance, I let my silence be the signal to tell me more.

"I'm tired of claiming God answers my prayers. I'm fed up hiding my doubts in silence. I'm weary of pretending this faith stuff is as real as I'm told it must be. Frankly, I wonder if I'm being duped. But whether I am or not, one thing is certain—some of the pieces are not fitting together. Sometimes I feel so shallow I start thinking about giving it all up."

When I did respond to Luke in words, there was no temptation to feel spiritually superior. Doubt has always been mixed with my faith in Christ. My years as a serious follower of Jesus have raised questions that continue to be unresolved. The interface between the theory of my faith and my behavior is still being examined. Sometimes my theory gets refined, while other times I must face the reality that some of my attitudes and behavior are simply sinful and unacceptable. Luke and I spent the rest of the evening probing each other's inner sanctuary.

I didn't understand everything that was going on that evening, but what Luke and I were trying to grapple with were some of the Christian enemies with smiling faces. His frustration with his faith and his anger toward God were rooted in well-intended assumptions about God and the gospel. But Luke's version of the faith was incomplete. It wasn't that it was totally wrong, but neither was it totally right. The church he was attending was not out to deceive him into believing he should always be able to discern how God answers prayer. His pastor never overtly taught, "Thou shalt always hide thy doubts." Still, Luke's faith community did nurture expectations and create fictitious images of reality that eventually turned on him. Too much of life was left unexamined. There was too much superficial goodness, too much rhetoric about victorious Christian living, too little honesty about the days and nights of real living.

People who live without regard for God live with vulnerabilities too. The world parades and preaches promises that form another ensemble of enemies with smiling faces. We live in times when it is easy to confuse dreams with reality. In the sober light of day we acknowledge that unending progress is in fact a myth. But technological advances, the dazzling allure of cyberspace, scientific breakthroughs and important medical findings all feed our expectations. We are affected. But when we are told that we can become whatever we want to be, that we can do all that we want to do, we are being set up for a tumble.

If we buy into the dream that first-class living is about having enough money to do whatever we want, whenever we want, wherever we want, with whomever we want, we will discover it is not enough. There is no virtue in lugging around the consequences of years of undisciplined eating. But although we feel better when we look better, losing weight does not transform us into new people. Success is a worthy aspiration, but we will pay too high a price if we end the day without self-respect. Sadly, life does not come stamped "satisfaction guaranteed or your money back."

Whether we live as Christians or people who have come to other conclusions about life, disappointment and dissatisfaction are not life's only destinations. God is present in the world. God has allies that we often do not recognize. But still the world is a dangerous place. It is dangerous because it invites its inhabitants to specialize in self-construction. And in the end, self-construction is a seductive enemy with a smiling face.

I don't believe there are easy answers to these harsh realities. But surely we can access a little more divine light for the rest of the journey. I continue to wonder: Why wasn't Craig wiser or more protected so as to end up less damaged? And surely it wasn't necessary for Luke to be so spiritually shattered, especially since he had such God-loving intentions.

Even though the world is a dangerous place, that's where we spend most of our time. God must want us to be as "wise as serpents and innocent as doves." Surely the God of creation, the resurrected Jesus and the guiding Spirit can grant us the discernment we need to deal with enemies with smiling faces.

God has used the Prayer of St. Francis to help me not only deal constructively with my struggles but also gain insight into the aspirations and anxieties of others. Thus phrases adapted from "Make Me an Instrument of Your Peace" introduce the four parts of this book. The array of enemies with smiling faces can be met with responses of prayer and invitation to live with new resolve, in the spirit of St. Francis:

Grant that I may seek not so much to believe as to discern.
Grant that I may seek not so much to be understood as to understand.
Grant that I may seek not so much to be right as to relate.
Grant that I may seek not so much to outwit as to outlove.

CHRISTIAN ENEMIES
WITH SMILING FACES

Grant that I may seek not so much
to believe as to discern.

Craig and Luke are not the only ones who live with vulnerabilities. I do and you do too. We cannot share life with other people and enjoy the prospect of being enriched without the risk of intrusive pain. Enemies with smiling faces inevitably lurk in the shadows of our lives.

But they do usually catch us off-guard. The damage dealt out by enemies with smiling faces is a lot like an injury received from friendly fire. The enemies who cause most pain are often the people or beliefs we expected to help us.

Sometimes family experiences are the cause of our grief. When families are the source of physical or emotional abuse, they become unexpected enemies. Spouses who turn their covenants to love and to be sexually faithful into instruments of betrayal are also unexpected enemies. Pain travels deep into the soul when friends take secrets whispered in confidence and spread them around as gossip. Neighbors who exploit our generosity, employers and employees who make promises to each other and then deliberately disregard them, and pastors and priests who preach with passion but live with intentional duplicity all have the potential of raining down friendly fire. And whether we are intentional targets or simply random victims of unscrupulous behavior, the experiences deliver throbbing pain.

I was born in western Canada on a small farm into a family that gifted me with a sense of security. I never once wondered whether my parents would be there for me. A part of the family package that I continue to value was a conservative religious upbringing. I suspect that my first public appearance was at church. Today I am less appreciative of all the legalistic trappings that were required to validate me as a follower of Jesus. They have been a blessing and a curse. On some occasions they protected me from self-destructing and pressed me to get reconnected with God. In too many ways, however, they twisted and marred my concept of God's grace. In one lifetime, no one should be subjected to the number of guilt trips that I have had to endure.

The good news is that God's grace and mercy are stronger and more creative than the tyranny of restrictive legalism. My religious training included an emphasis on daily quiet times. The biblical image of a deer coming early in the morning to drink from the life-giving stream of God's nurture was a part of my spiritual formation. Who can argue with the benefits to be derived from daily quiet times? However, I eventually came to realize I am not a deer, I am a camel! It turns out that I'm better off when I exchange daily spiritual drinking for extended sessions when I drink enough of God's good nourishment to last for a while.

Part one addresses Christian enemies with smiling faces. Whether we are basically satisfied with the state of our faith or wondering whether God is really accessible, my hope is that as we keep moving toward a more full-fledged faith, we will see the wisdom of praying, "Grant that I may seek not so much to believe as to discern."

1 Quick-Fix Faith

Being influenced by the world's invasive ways is a lot like catching a common cold. You wake up one day suddenly aware that something undesirable is happening to you. It is difficult to pinpoint the source of the problem. You reflect back on where you have been and whom you have been with. Could it be that the germs were simply in the air you breathed? You never really figure it out, but the sore throat, nose blowing and cough leave no doubt that you have a cold and there is no alternative but to keep the tissues handy.

Living in a world with germs can be a lot like living with the negative influences of the cultural forces that surround us, except that the world's presence can be a lot subtler and more consequential. The spirit of the age progressively moves in and takes up residence without creating discomfort. After all, many of the ways of the world are appealing, sensuous and downright desirable. Where we live has a profound impact on us; when we live wields power over us. As much as we may try to resist the cultural forces, they influence us. Society's norms get inside us, where we think, feel and dream.

I've actually tended to resist the notion that what we believe and how we behave is mainly the result of social conditioning. During my graduate school years I argued against deterministic theories that denied my personal prerogative to be more than the consequence of past experiences and present circumstances. Still, since then I've realized that although we make choices and have the capacity to resist social norms, we cannot escape being influenced, and sometimes we are simply engulfed by great cultural tides. Like it or not, we are all subject to cultural vulnerabilities, and committed church-attending Christians are especially susceptible to certain cultural influences that are enemies with smiling faces.

CULTURAL VULNERABILITY

The cultural tides that shape some of who we are and how we live gain access in different ways. Some Christians surrender to society's norms without putting up a fight, while others deliberately resist being embraced by these influences.

One way that God's people surrender is by isolating the sacred from the secular. These people appreciate Sunday worship, but their faith is not connected to Monday's routines. Such "spiritual isolators" make little effort to apply their faith to the demands of everyday life—particularly to their vocational worlds. Thus they end up being shaped by their immediate environments.

Other followers of Jesus resist the world's ways and intentionally integrate their faith into their choices and lifestyle. These "spiritual integrators" are like people who use a clearly marked map to get to their destination. They deliberately seek out God's direction. As parents, they are anxious to model the qualities they hope their children will embrace. As employers, they are more concerned about treating their staff fairly than about exploiting their staff's energies. As employees, they act with honesty and integrity whether anyone is looking or not. Spiritual integrators also welcome God into their leisure choices and community activities. They keep their hands on the steering wheel of their life.

But spiritual integrators can also be influenced by the sights and sounds of the world that surrounds them. Consciously or unconsciously, they can yield to the temptations of excessive ambition and the insatiable appetite for money. Spiritual integrators can be subject to self-interest that pushes others aside, and they can succumb to a pace of life that makes it almost impossible to slow down and listen to God's voice. Even with their hands firmly gripping the steering wheel, spiritual integrators can end up traveling off course.

I suspect that most Christians who tumble into cultural captivity do so unconsciously. They are neither spiritual isolators nor spiritual integrators. They go to work, pay their taxes, attend church, care for their neighbors, watch television, appreciate their leisure, breathe the air of the spirit of the age and become culturally shaped. And in doing so, they encounter enemies with smiling faces.

SPIRIT OF THE AGE CHANTS

Here's how it happens. The spirit of the age chants out its messages in image after image, advertisement after advertisement, encounter after encounter:

Demand less, permit more
Surrender less, control more
Consume more, pay less
Avoid pain, escape the mundane
Let your personal preferences reign.

The rhythm of such cultural chants seeps into the perceptions and expectations of those who are committed to follow Jesus. Both members of the clergy and people in church pews are influenced.

This cultural shaping has an effect on our faith. We start expecting to receive the benefits of a demand-less-permit-more, quick-fix faith. You won't pass churches with signs out front that announce: "Get your quick-fix faith here." But people do begin to adjust their expectations. The demands of discipleship are diminished, and a "more for less" mindset makes its way into individual and group life.

Gerrard Kelly, a social analyst from England, contends that "what is true in the marketplace of goods and services is spilling over into the marketplace of ideas, with philosophical and religious choices increasingly subject to the same consumer criteria."[1] Shades of what the world believes blend and blur their way into Christian beliefs. The desires and fickleness of consumers soften the demands of truth. The cultural practice of shopping for the lowest price transfers into seeking low-price, quick-fix faith. Over time, culturally induced quick-fix faith becomes a Christian enemy with a smiling face.

FAST FOOD SPIRITUALITY

North America is full of fast food franchises. Hamburgers and fries, chicken fingers and tacos are immediately accessible, and whether you are on the East Coast or the West Coast, it is pretty much guaranteed that they will taste the same. So why wouldn't we expect ready access to fast food spirituality—prepackaged and palatable, sating immediate hunger without nourishing the deep famine of the soul?

The inadequacy of fast food spirituality is that it has no strength to endure. Prepackaged faith is shallow faith. It feeds soft-mindedness. It prompts people to believe that "if it tastes good, it must be right."

Missiologist Lesslie Newbigin insists, "The effort to know the truth involves struggle, groping, feeling one's way. It is true that there are also moments of sudden illumination, but these come only to those who have accepted the discipline of patient groping, of trying out different possibilities, of sustained reflection."[2]

Illustrating another dimension of fast food spirituality, Dallas Willard observes that the American evangelical church is "guilty of making converts and not disciples. In so doing it perpetuates a great omission in the Great Commission."[3] Fast food spirituality produces faith "on the lite side," a casualty of the prevailing norms of current culture.

SHORTCUTS TO SUBSTANCE

Gratification *now!* That is what we are culturally conditioned to demand. And unfortunately, we often get it. The "gratification now" expectation in the spiritual arena means that moments of divine encounter get confused with the depth and substance of long-term commitment. Philosopher of religion Elton Trueblood laments, "The terrible danger of our time consists in the fact that ours is a cut flower civilization. Beautiful as cut flowers may be, and much as we may use our ingenuity to keep them looking fresh for a while, they will eventually die, and they die because they are severed from their sustaining roots."[4]

Quick-fix faith does not drive down deep spiritual roots. When we don't realize the value of developing an integrated faith, we are likely to live going from one experience to another. Often there is more form than substance. Researcher George H. Gallup Jr. observes that "mere church membership, for example, does not necessarily indicate authentic, transforming faith. Years of polls show scant difference between the churched and unchurched in terms of cheating, tax evasion, and pilferage."[5]

Authentic and transforming faith affirms "spiritual practices as journeys, not day trips into the realm of the sacred. They are not hobbies or occasional exercise."[6] Faith that has substance has strength. It embraces the demands of the journey.

As an antidote to teaching that is thin and faith that lacks substance, Old Testament scholar Stanley Hauerwas suggests provocatively that "the Bible is not and should not be accessible to merely anyone, but rather it should only be made available to those who have undergone the hard discipline of existing as part of God's people."[7] What I interpret Hauerwas to mean is that being a full-fledged member of God's faith family costs something. Understanding the Bible's meaning requires the disciplines of focus and reflection. We seldom access God's wisdom in an impromptu moment of personal insight. Rather, we do so by linking our lives with others who also nurture a vital and maturing faith.

You may want to resist the high-demand faith of Hauerwas, but be aware. Quick-fix faith is tantamount to a marriage without commitment. Unless the patterns change, the probability of spiritual divorce looms.

As Christian people, we are marked with good intentions. We are eager to believe what is right and good and true. Regrettably, committed Christians can be vulnerable people. We are vulnerable to overbelieving without discernment—to embracing and being embraced by teachers and practices of churches that eventually turn out to be smiling enemies of the soul.

Religious Magic Expectations

One expectation in many faith communities is that God works in a "religious magic" manner. Rooted in a right and deep belief that God performs miracles, this call of faith is "Heal me now, fix me forever!" God may well intervene, but unrealistic expectations coupled with an absence of sustained spiritual disciplines leave people vulnerable to returning to the same old long-term patterns.

Andrew's father told me the story of his son. Andrew had been raised in a Christian home, but he struggled with making faith a part of his life. His interests were often outside the church, and most of his friends had little regard for God. Still, Andrew's family relationships were positive, and he continued to be an insider at numerous church events.

Just prior to his senior year of high school, Andrew attended his church's summer camp. During an evening campfire, Andrew heard God's call to make a commitment and knelt at the outdoor altar. His struggle was honest and real. Andrew believed he could not be a good Christian without conquering his anger and uncontrolled temper. Confessing his concern to that evening's preacher, he was assured that if he would just surrender to Christ his temper would come under control.

Andrew returned home a different person. His parents were elated. They noted that Andrew had begun setting his wake-up alarm a few minutes early in order to have quiet time with God.

Then the countenance of Andrew's father darkened. "On the seventeenth day after Andrew came home from camp, we found his Bible and quiet time materials in his trash can. As far as we know he has never touched a Bible again. Years later we learned that on that day at school, Andrew had lost his temper on the basketball court."

Belief in religious magic puts God on the hook for more presence and more intervention than God promises. There is no biblical evidence that God places people in a cosmic microwave and zaps them with superhuman spiritual energy. New life in Christ is transformative, but it does not re-engineer our genes or radically alter our temperaments. In the end, belief in spiritual magic damages people.

OBEDIENCE TO THE PARTY LINE

A more subtle invitation to opt for quick-fix faith comes to Christian people in the multiple forms of organized religion. There is the Presbyterian, Pentecostal and Baptist fix. There is the Methodist, Lutheran and Mennonite fix. There is the Catholic, Anglican, Missionary Alliance and Church of God fix. As right and important as it is to become an active participant in a church faith community, uncritical involvement can amount to unexamined spiritual surrender.

The problem with unexamined spiritual surrender is precisely that it is unexamined. It is the difference between being present by default and being present by choice. "Default people" are just there. They follow the line of least resistance. They vote with the majority and go with the flow. They are ready to embrace and be embraced by the party line. Consequently, their church's brand of faith is their unexamined brand. It serves as their version of quick-fix faith.

In *The Habit of Being Catholic* novelist Flannery O'Connor wisely calls us to "learn what you can, but cultivate Christian skepticism. It will keep you free—not free to do anything you please, but free to be formed by something larger than your own intellect or the intellect of those around you."[8]

PERSONAL POWER

A closely related phenomenon is the excessive influence of pastoral entrepreneurs. Successful spiritual leaders can have difficulty distinguishing between cultivating personal converts and developing disciples of Jesus. Pastoral entrepreneurs are gifted, competent, confident and persuasive. They are often more inclined to be directly accountable to God than to their boards of deacons and trustees. But most of all, they are leaders. They cultivate loyalties and convince people to follow their ways. In response, overtrusting and nondiscerning people become vulnerable to the eventual costs of spiritual shortcuts. They succumb to this manifestation of quick-fix faith.

I'm not suggesting that pastoral entrepreneurs are driven by calculated motives to overcontrol. Most often they are products of our "personal power" age. People are looking for people to trust and believe in. However, even the pastors' innocence does not protect their followers from the dark side of their leadership style, the temptation toward merely vicarious faith.

Unfortunately, followers who line up behind their preacher heroes, those who take notes and enthusiastically cite their wisdom, tend to assimilate faith through their mighty leaders. They embody a faith that in significant measure belongs to someone else. In its extreme form, surrendering to the influence of personal power substitutes faith in a person for faith in our true God. And whenever human allegiances displace God, get ready to meet an enemy in disguise.

We can and should put faith in people. God lifts up and blesses people for good redemptive purposes. But every person has flaws. No one gets it all right—not even me. Excessive faith in people leads to inevitable disappointment. Leaders eventually move on to their next vision. Pastors make bad decisions that inflict damage on their parishioners. And now and then the people we trust are blatantly untrustworthy.

I know what it is like to be betrayed by a spiritual mentor. I respected him, was appreciatively subject to his strong influence and unconsciously attempted to emulate him. When proof came that for years he had hidden very deceptive and deviant behavior, I was crushed. I felt exploited and abused. I experienced waves of anger interspersed with empathy and then disgust. Eventually my anger and disappointment were replaced with forgiveness, but there is still spiritual scar tissue deep inside me. Today I can name a number of people who spiritually inspire me, but the inevitability of human limits keeps me turned toward God.

DIRECTION FOR THE JOURNEY

We will be wise to notice temptations to overbelieve and underdiscern. Whether the source of influence flows from a TV channel or a pulpit, we should be on guard. "Watch out for deceptive voices—worldly voices making promises, Christian voices calling for commitments that don't fit into Christ's will and ways. Beware of enemies with smiling faces" (Col 2:8 paraphrased).

Watch out for the incessant pressures of the culture that surrounds us. Be alert for the pressures that access our spirits in the churches where we worship. The warning is not just to live guardedly or defensively. It is also positive: Live with the expectation that God transcends the influence of both culture and church. Expect to be interrupted by God. Anticipate the presence of God crossing your path and altering your plans.[9] What we need is *God's* direction for living both in the world and in the church.

And when the way seems unclear and we are pushed and pressed, we can take time to pray quietly: "Grant that I may seek not so much to believe as to discern."

2 Feeling-Only Faith

It's confession time. I come from a cool, cold-in-the-winter country—and I'm not just talking about the temperature. Compared to many areas of the world, Canada is a spiritual ice zone. Even when we Canadians love God deeply, many of us tend to let our feelings hide inside our timid spirit.

I'm not saying that Canadians are without feeling or that emotional outbursts are culturally banned. Rather, our feelings are not the first voice we use to express ourselves. We are inclined to ponder before letting loose with exclamations or expressions of affection. And to be sure, our temperaments affect how we express, or remain reticent to express, our faith.

Let me speak for myself. I feel deeply about many matters. I can get angry reading the newspaper or watching the news on television. My spirit weeps when I meet women and children who are victims of HIV/AIDS. Every time someone tells me about yet another divorce or a premature death, anguish is unleashed inside me.

But although I treasure my friends, I find it difficult to say to them, "I love you." And when I'm with people who lavish love talk on me and others, I get uncomfortable. In church services and at weekend retreats I get tired of singing emotive worship songs over and over again. Before

long my mind takes over. I start thinking about the lyrics, and often—
undoubtedly too often—I become judgmental about what is apparently
spiritually inspiring to others.

There is a lot more going on inside me than gets expressed outside.
Maybe it's a generational thing. Or perhaps my natural bent is to think
before my feelings begin to stir. But please, grant me a little grace. I'm
simply saying that what seems to stir the feelings of others can shut mine
down.

I'm fearful that my confession may prompt you to skip this chapter.
Particularly in these times, I know that given a choice, many people
would prefer a heart massage over thinking about an idea that arouses
the mind. Still, I'm convinced that "feeling-only faith" will end up being
an enemy with a smiling face.

EXPERIENCE APPEALS

The spirit of the age is captured by sociologist Françoise Champion:
"What we look for today is personal experience. What counts is to feel
something. This new way of dealing with faith is not restricted to the
young."[1] Perhaps Pascal got it right: "It is the heart which experiences
God, and not reason. This, then, is faith: God felt by the heart, not by
reason."[2] If I personally experience God, is that the ultimate validation
of faith?

Seeker-sensitive churches are reading the desire for experience as the
critical faith issue in these times. They are

> responding to a religious environment characterized by subjectiv-
> ism, expanding religious choice, eclectic spirituality, and anti-insti-
> tutionalism. . . . The assumption is that churches that offer an ex-
> citing, vital experience of the sacred can win the loyalty of seekers.
> To this end, they make use of contemporary music, multimedia
> presentations, screens, and drama.[3]

And clearly God is at work in this milieu. More than just attracting people's attention, worship, drama, dance and symbolism awaken the spirit
and capture many people's hearts. People are responding to the spiritual

appeal to seek experiences of God for themselves, and God's presence energizes them. But will the energy wane and the heart go looking somewhere else for another kind of experience?

DEMISE OF DOCTRINE

When a cultural or religious movement goes somewhere new, it leaves something old behind. As many have observed, today's emphasis on experience is partly explained by the decline of the rational. And without a doubt, the increasing distrust in reason is pushing Christian doctrine off its historically lofty perch.

An interview with Sven Birkerts suggests how far away many serious Christians have moved from a focus on objective truth. "Wisdom for me," claims Birkerts, "is understanding that has been derived largely through experience, and the pondering of experience as opposed to understanding, which has been derived from the reading of wise things."[4]

Theologian Michael Horban notes, "Much of the phenomena associated with present-day renewal movement is without any clear biblical foundation. . . . We assume that because these things are happening to Christians, and they feel good about their experience, . . . it must be from God." But then he warns, "Not always."[5]

The nature of faith itself is in transition. The decline of trust in rational reality and the ascent of the affective mean that we are high on the heart and low on the mind. The swinging of the pendulum toward feeling crashes into the desire to think.

Norman Lamm, Yeshiva University president, believes that eventually we will find a balance, giving equal credence to a subjective spirituality "and a more structured religious life based on conduct and behavior in the ritual, ethical, moral, and social realms."[6]

In the meantime, we can expect many churches to downplay the rule of doctrine and theology as they emphasize the subjective rewards of faith. Humor will become a necessary part of ritual, atmospheres will be relaxed and casual, and theology will be kinder, gentler and inoffensive.[7] Along the way, the demise of doctrine will continue with hardly anyone paying tribute to its important role and contribution.

FEELINGS ARE ESSENTIAL

It is unfortunate that during the reign of rationalism many leaders of organized religious life were not able to grasp the concept that feelings were essential too. Christian traditions that did not emphasize the activity of the Holy Spirit focused their version of Christianity on the virtue of understanding the faith. The logic was impeccable. It was necessary to know about the faith in order to know God. And in order to explain the faith to others, you first had to understand the faith yourself.

I reflected on how differently the faith is being framed today while listening to Bishop Robinson Cavalcanti, an Anglican from Brazil. He caught my attention by claiming, "The human spirit needs mystical food for the soul. In the long term, there is no faith without mystery. Christianity without mystery is fatal. . . . The journey of faith is to keep searching for the mystery."[8] Obviously, the human spirit is hungry for more than propositions. And could it be that dogma is often delivered with a dogmatic tone? The tragic reality is that by failing to affirm the importance of feelings, those who propagated the centrality of right doctrine set themselves up for failure.

Our hearts do ache for a divine presence. There is no argument. In order for our faith to be real, to be personal, we do need to feel Jesus present with us. But is feeling the presence of Jesus enough?

FEELINGS ARE NOT ENOUGH

I love eating cashew nuts, especially salted dry roasted cashews. Cashews should be eaten one at a time: their tenderness carefully crunched, their flavors savored slowly. But as much as I enjoy my cashew experiences, I tire of them quickly. Once I've had six or maybe eight, I stop appreciating how good they really are.

Feeling-only faith is like living on a "cashew only" diet. It's a great taste experience that just won't quit. Blocking out the desire for other kinds of spiritual food, the cashew high fuels an unending desire for more and more of the same.

Followers of Jesus who restrict their spiritual diet to feeling-only faith end up neglecting their mind. Instead of seeking the substance of ideas, the temptation is to live on sensations. The faith gets dumbed down to the emotive, and the rich experiences that flow out of loving God with our mind are simply absent. Overindulgence in experiential faith for the heart without the balance of faith for the mind produces a diet of Christian comfort food. The Scriptures spell out the consequences: "Solid food is for the mature, for those whose faculties have been trained by practice to distinguish good from evil" (Heb 5:14). Unfortunately, there can be no discernment without insight, no eloquence without substance, no passionate communication without the presence of ideas.

Paul Wilke articulates the completeness many of us desire: "We need a divine presence, here and now, in our present condition. We need a Jesus in the home, on the street, on the job, in the community and world—as well as a Jesus in church or private prayer. We need a Jesus who is consistent, and yet able—and who can help us to be able—to deal with the inconsistencies and ever-changing circumstances of life."[9]

FEELINGS BLOCK OUT OTHERS

Followers of Jesus who focus on spiritual experiences are oriented to enjoy God. Celebratory worship is their spiritual lifeline. They don't consciously say, "I won't engage my mind until the benediction has been pronounced." They simply want to be open to receive what God gives.

Feeling-only Christians do live with vulnerabilities, however. One temptation is to become so focused on one's own experience that it is difficult to make room for others. The essential corporate nature of the Lord's Prayer is lost, and what remains is

My Father who art in heaven . . .
Lead me not into temptation . . .
Deliver me from evil . . .

The smiling face of feeling-only faith can hide unintentional selfishness. "Genuine spirituality makes demands on us, challenges us to overcome selfishness, to love from the depths of ourselves so that we may establish community with others despite our sinful human condition," asserts Eugene Kelley. Otherwise we are "more about shadow than substance."[10]

Living with insight and sensitivity toward others is not a simple matter. Responding appropriately to those who are dealing with difficult circumstances can be profoundly challenging—especially if clear Christian thinking hasn't preceded the encounter.

I will always remember the day I was sitting at our kitchen table and the phone rang with the traumatic news that a van loaded with InterVarsity students had just been in a head-on collision with a semi-trailer truck. Staff member Mike and a student had been killed. Two other young women were being airlifted to a major hospital with life-threatening injuries that would eventually leave them with serious disabilities. I directed InterVarsity in the region and was responsible for responding to the tragedy.

Mike left behind a two-month-old son. His wife, Catherine, was devastated, as were the parents of the student who had been killed. I spent the next few days arranging pastoral care for students in the hospital, helping to plan funerals and writing eulogies.

A few days after Mike's funeral, I met with Catherine again. She was grieving deeply, but she was also extremely distraught. "You will never believe what Christian people have been saying to me, Don. I know they mean well, but they are not helpful, they are cruel."

"What have you been hearing?" I asked.

"I've been told, 'God's will is never wrong . . . I know it's hard right now, but all things do work together for good . . . We have to trust that God is still in charge . . . What you can be sure of is that Mike is with the Lord.'" With tears flowing freely, Catherine lamented, "For God's sake, I'm alone with a two-month-old son, and I don't have a husband to make me laugh or hold me and say, 'I love you.'"[11]

There are times for exhortations to trust God, but Catherine's situation was not one of them. It would have been far better for friends to stay silent or simply to say, "Your pain must be unbearable. I will keep praying for you." Or if it was appropriate, "When you need a babysitter, I'm available."

Of course some people have more social sensitivities and interpersonal skills than others. We need to make allowances. But thoughtless use of the words of Scripture and faith damages people. Unreflective reciting of religious rhetoric is demeaning to God. Traumatic times are occasions to think with a clear Christian mind. Although feeling-only Christians have the right intentions, they lack capacity to think with clarity.

Mike was one of the few people I knew who had the gift of evangelism. The students in the van had been headed for an evangelistic outreach ski weekend. It's been over a decade now, and I still can't find any divine purpose in the tragedy.

Please don't ask me to believe that all that pain and suffering was God's preferred will. I can accept the reality that God permitted the natural laws of life to rule. Under the physical laws of the created order, when a small van collides with a semi-trailer truck, the truck wins. But acknowledging this is far different from attributing the tragedy to "God's will."

FULLY ALIVE

Recently my responsibilities as World Vision's director for church relations took me to Uganda. On the flight home I found myself sitting next to a woman who was reading her Bible and praying privately. When it seemed appropriate, I introduced myself and asked what church she attended. She smiled and explained that she had been born into a Catholic family, had married an Anglican and was now attending a charismatic church. Her name was Cecelia; she was a member of the Ugandan parliament and had a long history of social activism. Flashing a broad smile, she said, "I'm a member of the government at this point, but my colleagues tell me that I'm their internal member of the opposition."

Cecelia used the word *justice* often. "We now have a policy of primary school for all children, but if we can't also help them acquire vocational skills, we will have failed the young ones. And equal opportunity for girls and women continues to be a challenge for us." After talking about the long-standing conflict with the Lord's Resistance Army in Northern Uganda, Cecelia's face clouded. "I don't understand why our churches aren't more involved in helping us restore peace. Why don't they at least pray more about the trouble?"

In 1995 Uganda's president had invited her to serve as his vice president. "We discussed the issue on several occasions, but finally I said to the president, 'If I join you, what will happen to my voice? I'm afraid I will lose my freedom to fight for the values and principles of justice that are important to me.' In the end I said no to his request. And my voice is still free."

Cecelia's vibrant faith, alert mind and strong will deserve to be emulated. Her life is "rooted and grounded in love" (Eph 3:17). Her life in Christ has brought her "breadth and length and height and depth . . . that surpasses knowledge" (vv. 18-19). She is fully alive.

We are all meant to be partners with the God of the universe. We are meant to be contributors to the divine plan for our world, aware of each other and ready to act in response to each other's needs. Too often people who are caught up savoring their last spiritual experience and anticipating their next encounter with God's Spirit have not developed the mind of Christ so that they can respond insightfully to injustice, oppression and pain.

PREEMPTING COMPLETENESS

"Jesus increased in wisdom and in years, and in divine and human favor" (Lk 2:52). He grew up to be a full-fledged person. Jesus developed physically in years, mentally in wisdom, socially in human favor and spiritually in divine favor. He was a thinking, feeling, relating and spiritually alive whole person. His healthy wholeness is central to the example Jesus offers to the rest of us.

Life gets off track when we tumble into excesses. Too many cashews, too much emotion, too much self, too much thinking and even excessive concern for others can all be destructive in the end. We are created for healthy wholeness, and when we overindulge one area of life, other parts of ourselves are stifled. We remain crippled, incomplete, rather than whole.

Feeling-only faith cripples people because it is incomplete. Overindulging the experiential and emotive parts of life, it denies the development of other realms. Spirituality that incites emotional responses is often offered as relief from mundane routines or a way to avoid life's pain. Rather than looking into the face of reality and dealing directly with suffering, feeling-only faith is likely to counsel, "Jesus is all I need."

Jesus is all we need *only* when he is allowed to touch all of our life. That includes the darkness as well as the light, despair as well as hope, pain as well as pleasure. Stanley Crouch is right: "The big problem with most organized religion is the way it evades recognition of the pain at the center of trying to live a religious life—which means, finally, a life that's humane."[12] Feeling-only faith parades Easter celebration without Good Friday suffering. And when its practices nurture an incomplete faith, it is an enemy with a smiling face.

DIRECTION FOR THE JOURNEY

Christian faith encompasses all of life. It is about entering into a relationship with the God of the universe, who, improbable as it sounds, wants to be present in all of life with us. This all-knowing God also desires that the people who grace the universe will experience healthy wholeness, that those who have experienced re-creation in Christ and share touches of his likeness will live as fully alive, whole people.

Accordingly, rather than restricting God to worship that energizes the spirit or to contemplation that quietly inspires, we invite God into all of life:

- the darkness of the soul as well as the light
- the private and the public
- the personal and the social
- the parties and the pain
- the mundane
- the days and nights of reality

Welcoming the loving God into all of our reality allows us to make our way toward as much completeness as can be found this side of heaven's door.

Grant that I may seek not so much to believe as to discern.

3 One-Sided Faith

Recently I shared a Canadian platform and podium with a prominent evangelical writer and speaker from the United States. The special worship celebration was held in a large hockey arena. He was the American headliner to bring in the crowds. I was the Canadian speaker to give the event national content.

My appreciation of the creativity and substance of his writing motivated me to carefully tune in to the content of his address. I was on track with everything until I heard the statement "It's not the job of the church to clean up the world." My interest heightened. After emphasizing the mandate of the church to call people into a saving personal relationship with Christ, he again proclaimed, "It's not the job of the church to clean up the world." I thought, *Our lunchtime conversation will be stimulating.*

Join me for another conference experience, this one in East Africa. The venue was a vocational school. The conference involved a broad spectrum of church leaders from sub-Saharan Africa and decision-makers from the World Bank. The purpose was to explore ways the World Bank could link with churches as community development partners.

Early every morning there was an optional devotional gathering. It was like a scaled-down church service. There was time for singing, a brief homily, prayer and celebration of the Eucharist. One day I had arrived a little late and was sitting at the back of the auditorium when it came time for people to participate in prayer.

People expressed themselves in ways you would expect in that culturally diverse and denominationally mixed setting. Then suddenly a man began to call out his petitions in a firm, zealous voice. He prayed passionately that Christ would enter into us anew, that Jesus would forgive us, that the Lord of history would overrule us and that the blood of the cross would cleanse us. His prayer focused on Christ and nothing else.

Moments of silence followed that prayer of exhortation. Then in a much quieter voice, a woman began to pray. "God, you are the Creator and Sustainer of our broken world. You long to be with us, and sometimes we don't even take time to listen to you. Forgive us. O God, please care for your creation today. Give people enough food to eat. May children who want to go to school find enough money to pay their fees. And God, we pray that our government leaders would not yield to the temptation of corruption today or in the future. Amen."

The two prayers intrigued me, captured my mind and yet troubled my spirit. It was like they were speaking two different languages and praying to two different Gods. As I walked across the campus I thought, *Those two followers of Jesus need each other.* One would benefit from the passion flowing from a personal focus on Christ, and the other needs the compassionate touch of the loving God who agonizes over the plight of broken humanity.

Just as personal faith without social action faith is an enemy with a smiling face, so is social action faith without the energizing presence of personal faith.

THE PREDICAMENT

The lunch discussion with my speaking colleague at the Canadian gathering was helpful. Offering sincere commendation for his fresh insights, I went on to ask for clarification on his statement, "It's not the job of the church to clean up the world." He talked about slavery as a social problem in New Testament times and contended that Jesus did little to address the situation. I agreed that the primary focus of the Bible is not that particular issue, but I asked how, in more general terms, he understood the overall mission of the church. "How do you interpret the biblical call for justice? Is God just concerned about personal salvation, or do we dare to dream of the restoration of creation? Is it possible that God is calling the church to work toward re-creating what God hoped for in the very beginning?"

Ron Sider, a long-time advocate of the biblical necessity of both personal faith and social action, defines the problem:

> Most churches today are one-sided disasters. In some suburban churches hundreds of people come to Jesus and praise God in brand-new buildings, but they seldom learn that their new faith has anything to do with wrenching inner-city poverty just a few miles away. In other churches the members write their senators and lobby the mayor's office, but they understand little about the daily presence of the Holy Spirit. They would be stunned if someone asked them to invite their neighbors to accept Christ.[1]

Personal faith and social faith churches hold different views on how to create a better world. Conservative evangelical churches are inclined to see sin, evil and people in need through an individualistic lens. The problem as this segment of God's family sees it is people's alienation from Christ and God's good ways. If people will only come to Christ and be converted and changed, then they will live in wholesome and honorable ways. Selfish people will become generous, criminals will live as law-abiding citizens, and emotionally imbalanced people will be healed. The strategy is to root out personal problems, and in the process social problems will be resolved.

Socially minded churches tend to view their deeds of faith as ends in themselves. Expressing love and doing good is the true form of preaching. They "insist that the battle against sin must be waged against inequities and injustices in the social order that twist the personal lives of individuals and do violence to their high status as creatures made in the image of God."[2]

People in the two kinds of churches live with different visions of the same faith. One group believes that personal conversion and saving souls are paramount. The other group believes the Christian faith is essentially about serving the needs of others. These churches often become polarized from each other and fracture the kingdom of God. And tragically, both types of faith communities are limited to living out a partial gospel. One celebrates conversions without holistic discipleship, the other emphasizes social action without seeking the sustaining energy of God's personal presence.

Why does this predicament exist? The thing is, both sides of the gospel—the personal and the social—are so potent, so right and so persuasive that each has the strength to stand on its own. Of course there are historical and theological reasons that some churches gravitate to either faith that is personal or faith that is social, but one reason they stay in a single track is the profound richness of the gospel. The faith is so forceful and consequential that even without believing and experiencing both sides of the gospel equation, one can find significant levels of credibility and satisfaction.

Let's consider the compelling strengths of each side of the faith.

RESTORING RELATIONSHIP

People who have lived with little or no regard for God and then have a personal encounter with Christ can be captivated by their experience. The power of confession, the dynamics of forgiveness and the hope of living in new ways are enthralling. It is no wonder that people who taste and see that Jesus is who he claims to be are ready to settle in and look for more of what they have already experienced.

A friend's family story illustrates the life-changing impact of personally encountering Christ. Barry was raised in what used to be a conventional North American home. Dad went to work in the morning and came home to a supper table that often featured his favorite food. Mom's domain was the home, and that included the role of being the primary parent. The kids went to school, enjoyed their friends, played some sports and began developing their own interests. On Sunday the family went to church together.

Life for the family kept pretty much on course until Barry's younger brother, Andrew, left to attend university. At the end of his second year, Andrew announced that he was going to take time off from his studies to travel the world. Although there was a phone call back home to Mom and Dad once or twice a year after that, Andrew essentially disconnected and disappeared.

During the absent years I periodically heard Barry lament, "It wasn't that I was his best friend, but he's the only brother I have. There's a part of me that seems to be missing." As the years passed and no one in the family had any contact with Andrew, Barry's lament turned into grieving: "I wonder if Andrew is still alive."

One day Mom picked up the phone at the family home. It was a call from Andrew. He didn't really apologize but said he wanted to come home so his parents could meet his wife and their new grandson.

By this time Barry lived more than a thousand miles away from the family home, and a few weeks passed before there was a reunion. That was when I got a call from Barry. With some apprehension in his voice, he told me the story and the prospect of good news: "My brother Andrew and I are going to get reconnected."

Today Barry's and Andrew's families have vacation properties next door to each other. They go fishing together, sit on each other's deck, discuss issues that matter, celebrate birthdays and anniversaries, absorb each other's pain and disappointments, laugh a lot and treasure their relationship. They never did detail what happened during the absent years. They just started again.

Faith on the personal side of the gospel equation is about reconnecting. It is exchanging absence for presence, silence for communication. Without the necessity of replaying the past, faith in Christ involves spending time in the present—both pain time and party time. Life with Christ connects worship and work, the pleasure of vacation and the repetitiveness of mundane chores.

Following Jesus is an embrace of the known and the unknown in the ebb and flow of a relationship meant to endure. Sometimes when the relationship goes bad, it needs to start again. And it can start again by believing again. "For God so loved the world that he gave his only Son, so that everyone who believes in him may not perish but may have eternal life" (Jn 3:16).

People who experience a restored relationship with God and are re-created in Christ Jesus have an inside track on discerning God's ways. Some of God's ways are straightforward and obvious. They are like the physical laws of the universe. The law of gravity means that we will be severely injured or possibly killed if we jump off a ten-story building and fall on the pavement below. Contravening God's moral laws has the same disastrous consequences. When we repeatedly dismiss God's law of love, we become dismal human beings. Whether we believe it or not is irrelevant. As an antithesis to a life of love, unrestrained selfishness is toxic. When selfishness pushes aside the practice of love, it poisons environments, destroys people and contaminates whatever it touches.

God's ideas and God's ways are not always evident. Even the timeless and transcultural Scriptures leave room for human discovery, the generation of multiple points of view on the same idea. But God's ideas and preferences are there to be discerned. Whether the subject matter is ethics or values, social issues or moral dilemmas, justice concerns or family matters, lifestyle choices or vocational challenges, divine direction is etched into the framework of God's creation. And those who are re-created in Christ Jesus have spiritual eyes to see and spiritual ears to hear. Within our faith communities and in times of personal reflection, we are prompted to search the Scriptures and surrender to the whispers of the Holy Spirit.

THE NEED FOR TWO-SIDED FAITH

Those of us who respond to Jesus' invitation to "come unto me" not only get reconnected with the God of the universe and increase our capacity to discern God's ideas but also receive the gift of the Spirit's continuing personal presence. God is saying, "I'd like to join you on life's journey. What do you think about traveling together?"

The ages and stages of a normal lifetime bring possibilities for many different kinds of trips. They will inevitably involve times that are good and bad, some days filled with light and others with darkness. There will be successes and failures, laughter and tears, right and wrong choices. In some situations spiritual obedience will prevail, and in others disobedience will invade. When we approach some intersections, the way ahead will be abundantly clear. At other intersections there will be no signs and no sense of guidance. At those perilous times, God will be there and the assurance of God's personal presence will be enough.

Still, though personal faith is transforming and treasured, on its own it is inadequate and even unbiblical. This reality was impressed on me while I was watching a BBC television feature on religious life in El Salvador.

Like other countries in Central and South America, El Salvador's religious life is dominated by the Catholic Church. The well-known tragedy of Catholic martyr Oscar Romero is a part of that presence. Known as an advocate of the poor who encouraged challenges to the systemic structures in his country, Father Romero was gunned down while celebrating the Eucharist.

The television documentary focused on what the commentators labeled the "invasion into El Salvador of evangelical cults." As a result, "now there are churches on every corner." The commentators delineated differences between evangelical churches and the Catholic commitment to the social gospel. When the tension was presented to an evangelical pastor, he responded: "There are two kinds of poor in the world, material poor and spiritual poor. There will always be the material poor with us. We can't do anything about that. But we can look after the spiritual poor."[3]

He was echoing my colleague on the coliseum platform: "It's not the job of the church to clean up the world." But personal faith without social action faith leaves us with an impoverished gospel. It not only lacks biblical integrity, it is a Christian enemy with a smiling face.

Historian Mark Noll says that in complex times like ours evangelicals "either mount a public crusade, or we retreat into an inner pious sanctum."[4] Raising awareness through a public crusade can have merit, but keeping Jesus in privatized piety leads to escapism. The practice disconnects faith from life. William Willimon reminds us to reforge the connection: "The gospel is intrusive news that evokes a new set of practices, a complex of habits, and a way of living in the world."[5]

EMPATHY AND INTIMACY

In the early 1950s, personal faith churches and social faith churches were theologically and organizationally divided from each other. Bob Pierce, the founder of World Vision, was able to bridge the distance between the two polarized approaches. An entrepreneurial evangelist with a heart for needy children, Pierce linked passion for personal faith with passion for the deeds of social faith.

Pierce's spirit was marked by empathy, particularly empathy for vulnerable children. In Korea, having somehow secured accreditation as a war correspondent, he worked amidst the appalling suffering of a country torn apart by war. There he wrote the words in the flyleaf of his Bible that were to become his life's theme: "Let my heart be broken by the things that break the heart of God."[6] Touched deeply by the suffering Christ of the cross, Pierce reached out to touch those who were also suffering.

Although the list of the fruits of the Spirit in Galatians does not include "empathy," personal faith that does not produce such concern for others is unfinished and incomplete. On the other side of the ledger, social faith that is not rooted in personal faith will struggle to endure. Dependent on human energy alone, the motivation to carry out deeds of social faith will tend to fade and falter over time.

There is tremendous power in personal presence. Regardless of what a caregiver believes, the presence of a person holding the hand of someone in emotional or physical pain is profound. When the caregiver is seeking to bring the presence of Christ into the predicament, the experience is redemptive. God is there absorbing the pain.

A long-time advocate for the poor, Carl Dudley speaks out of experience of the power of the personal. "When poverty wears a child's face, when a friend is unemployed, when the children or the elderly or the broken families are real to us—then, by the strange power of the Holy Spirit, their pain may trigger the necessary energy and endurance in us to organize a ministry in response. As one church member discovered, 'it hurts more when you know their names.' "[7]

People who become part of a community of faith that gives them opportunities to serve the needs of others in the name of Christ experience the presence of God through their service. In God's economy, people who give also receive.

Expressing social faith feeds the soul. Unfortunately, the strengths inherent in social faith create the potential for that one dimension of the gospel to become the only one that receives deliberate affirmation.

BEING THE HANDS AND FEET OF GOD

Focusing on just part of God's revelation is a common practice. "In recent years," writes cultural analyst John Drane, "I have gradually been moving towards the conclusion that our words are getting in the way of the gospel—that the church is somehow imprisoned in a kind of cognitive captivity which is inhibiting our mission."[8] Ideas and words without accompanying deeds lack credibility.

In our day the invasive barrage of the media means it is impossible to escape the sights or sounds of words. Every day we see and hear more messages than we can assimilate, let alone decide which messages merit serious consideration. No wonder many people are concluding, "The only way people will know what God is like is when they see Him at work."[9]

Some congregations act out their biblical faith more than they express it in the language of theoretical theology. They prefer to point to their actions rather than articulate their faith. The Millard Congregational United Church of Christ is an example: "We are not a posturing church. We let our deeds do the talking. We are forever mindful that we are God's hands and feet on earth. We don't have to be God's mouth. We strive humbly to love by serving, to teach by doing, and to preach by being. That is our theology."[10]

The congregation's commitment is a theology of active love that is mandated by the Scriptures: "We know love by this, that he laid down his life for us—and we ought to lay down our lives for one another. How does God's love abide in anyone who has the world's goods and sees a brother or sister in need and yet refuses help? Little children, let us love, not in word or speech, but in truth and action" (1 Jn 3:16-18).

But as virtuous as service and justice ministries are, when personal faith is not affirmed as well, people are left with an impoverished gospel. In the end, activism without Christ's personal presence leads to tiredness, and tiredness slumps into burnout. Burnout can push people to opt out. Personal and church tragedies result when what started as well-intentioned empathy shifts into withdrawal from people and good desires turn into personal bitterness.

To separate the two sides of personal and social faith from each other as I have done here is, of course, an overstatement. In reality, most congregations give some weight to both sides. Still, when either personal faith or social faith is affirmed to the neglect of the other, both faith orientations become enemies with smiling faces.

DIRECTION FOR THE JOURNEY

E. Stanley Jones is credited with the insight that "an individual gospel without a social gospel is a soul without a body, and a social gospel without an individual gospel is a body without a soul. One is a ghost and the other is a corpse."

Speaking with a prophetic voice, Sider warns that we often weaken or even destroy the transforming power of genuine conversion when we remain one-sided, by focusing exclusively on its vertical or horizontal dimension, by neglecting the social or the personal side of sin, by failing to see that love for God is inseparable from (but not identical with) love for neighbor.[11]

Vernon Grounds's definition will help us stay on track: "The church . . . is that community which prayerfully struggles to translate Paul's eulogy of love in 1 Corinthians 13 from poetry to practice."[12] Translating poetry into practice will keep us in a state of discovery. Taking steps from the known into the mysterious unknown will keep us close to the God of our faith. Otherwise the life-giving patterns of the past would be reduced to lifeless reruns, and what is old would grow cold.

We will be wise to remain modest and compassionate in our expectations for both others and ourselves. Richard Mouw, now president of Fuller Seminary, remembers an encounter with renowned sociologist Peter Berger. Idealistic and energetic, Mouw gave a talk in which he leveled a challenge: "Every Christian is called to engage in radical obedience to God's program of justice, righteousness and peace."

In a later conversation Berger challenged Mouw: "You seem to have a rather grandiose notion of 'radical obedience.' Somewhere in a retirement home there is a woman whose greatest fear in life is that she will be humiliated by being unable to control her bladder in a cafeteria line. For this woman, the greatest act of radical obedience to Jesus Christ is to place herself in the hands of a loving God every time she goes off for a meal."[13]

Theories of faith—including the ideal of faith that is both personal and social—need to be subject to the realities of life. I suspect that even when our theory celebrates both sides of the gospel equation, our best intentions leave us leaning to one side or the other. Thus we are wise to extend mercy to ourselves and also to others as we continue to pray, "Gracious God, grant that I may seek not so much to believe as to discern."

4 Spiritual Superiority

Sabbath saints are not my favorite kind of religious people. They are more predisposed to pronounce than to listen, more inclined to judge than to extend acceptance. Sabbath saints are too sure of themselves and are quite convinced that if I don't see life from their point of view, they are right and I am wrong. Even when the differences seem minor, they feel it is necessary to right the wrong. My one consolation is that Jesus' experience with sabbath saints didn't inspire him either.

The incident in John 5 at the Pool of Bethesda finds both Jesus and the man he healed being confronted with criticism from sabbath saints. The situation is preposterous. The man had been sick for thirty-eight years. Jesus approached with a question more important than "Do you want to be a millionaire?" He asked the man, "Do you want to be healed?" After an exchange between the two, Jesus miraculously healed the man, commanding him, "Stand up, take your mat and walk."

The trigger for the confrontation with the sabbath purists is that the healing took place on the sabbath and there are rules against such actions. First they take aim at the healed man: "You are carrying your mat on a 'Thou shalt not work' day." Then they turn their attack on Jesus:

"How dare you heal on the sabbath? Have you no respect for the law? What a vile thing to do!"

Jesus and sabbath saints look at life through different windows. Jesus is a life-giver, sabbath saints are life-deniers. Jesus' vision for life extends beyond the limits of the present to what the future can bring. Jesus responds to pain with compassion and celebrates the miracle, while sabbath saints lock themselves in legalistic prisons. And there is a consequence. They miss the party at the pool.

My critique of sabbath saints flows out of the biases of my own faith perspective. While Christian sabbath saints do not reflect my preferences for how to express faith, they have a right to their particular views. And not only do they have the same rights as other Christians, but sabbath saints also have virtues. Their intentions are honorable, and they can be counted on to stay faithful to their convictions.

The admission regarding my biases and assumptions also applies to another segment of religious people who confuse me. They are the "humanist saints." These are Christians who deep down do not believe in the possibility of miracles. Their cherished liberal beliefs motivate them to be outstanding humanists, but with the limits they place on God they also lock themselves in spiritual handcuffs. Humanist saints miss the party at the pool too.

While most humanist saints are easier to enjoy than sabbath saints, I struggle to comprehend their spirituality, especially when they parade their views with an air of intellectual superiority. Although I try hard to see life from the other person's point of view, I do not really understand why some religious people aren't more religious. Why would people who affirm belief in God as Creator of our remarkable world resist believing in miracles?

It just doesn't make sense to me to believe in a pale God. Why bother with tidbit faith, a little selection of moral appetizers? Why settle for faith etched in stained-glass sociology when you could build your life on the substance of grounded biblical beliefs and a shared experience in Christ? Stephen Carter states the case clearly: "To be devoutly religious, after all, is to believe in some aspect of the supernatural, whether the belief involves a certainty that God parted the Red Sea so that the Israelites could escape, or a conviction that Jesus Christ is the Son of God and rules the universe as part of the Holy Trinity."[1]

There are two major roads to travel on the way to spiritual superiority. Sabbath saints take the road that has reinforced guardrails, directional signs at every turn and hardly an intersection without traffic lights. They are genuinely convinced that their road is the only route to God's destination. They have the truth, their theology triumphs, their doctrines are pure, their personal convictions are all biblically defensible. They are so right and so committed to their right views that they hardly need any faith to believe. Who needs faith when you have more answers than questions?

Although it may not be apparent at first glance, humanist saints on the road to spiritual superiority have a lot in common with sabbath saints. The reason similarities might be missed is that on the road of the humanist saint there are no guardrails, and only a few signs and traffic lights appear here and there. But when you look and listen more closely, you realize the humanist saints believe intensely that they are right too. They are not as ready to make as many claims of certainty as the sabbath saints, but they are quite convinced about what cannot be claimed. What Christian orthodoxy has affirmed over the centuries, humanistic saints stamp with doubt: the authority of the Scriptures, the reality of the miraculous, the uniqueness of Christ, the virgin birth, the resurrection. Humanist saints stain the historic fundamentals of the faith with question marks. They have the truth about what cannot be known for sure.

If the Christian call is to be "the aroma of Christ" (2 Cor 2:15), then followers of Jesus who parade their spiritual superiority do more than give God a bad reputation. Particularly in this age, spiritual superiority emits a foul odor. Judgmental and condemning attitudes chase people away from Christ and the cross. And whether one stands on a spiritual perch as a sabbath saint or a humanist saint, enemies with smiling faces are hovering nearby.

Central to the temptation toward spiritual superiority is how we view the nature of God's truth. The question is not about the existence of truth or whether God has revealed truth to us. Rather, the question revolves around our human capacity to accurately discern the complexities of God's truth. There are reasons some people have greater capacities than others.

HISTORICAL NEGLECT

Debate and division have always marked the people of God. The apostle Paul would not have been the most prolific author in the New Testament were it not for a great array of problems among the early Christians. The ten centuries of dominance of the Church of Rome, the separation of the Orthodox Church in the eleventh century, the voices of dissent of the Protestant Reformation four centuries later and the endless splintering of the church from then until now make up a story of human struggle to faithfully know God's will and ways.

Discounting Christian differences will not lead to increased understanding and unity; neither will we move forward by ignoring the historical patterns. Surely one lesson we can learn from the past is that no single organized group of Christian believers has ever got it all right. Diversity of theological conviction and doctrinal commitments is simply part of the makeup of the extended Christian family of believers. Historian Edmund Morgan observes that "change in Christian thought, even so radical a change as the Reformation, has usually been a matter of emphasis, of giving certain ideas a greater weight than was previously accorded them or of carrying one idea to its logical conclusion at the expense of another."[2]

Accepting that Christian diversity is a matter of emphasis is not the same as proposing that all differences have equal significance. Obviously some areas of disagreement are more consequential than others. Discerning what is major and what is minor will always be crucial, but the inescapable reality is that "Christians who arm themselves with truth and righteousness will not necessarily come to the same conclusions, even if they are committed to common principles and have a good grasp of the situation."[3]

The Scriptures offer guidance and invite reflection: "Stand at the crossroads and look; ask for the ancient paths, ask where the good way is, and walk in it, and you will find rest for your souls" (Jer 6:16 NIV).

CLOSED SYSTEM THINKING

Larry Christenson illustrates how all Christians with strong convictions work from established frameworks. Using evangelicals and social activists as examples, he contends that "both operate within the same mentality: within a theological box, a closed system of ready-made answers, with little understanding or regard for other points-of-view. The evangelical has his set of texts, centering on personal experience of salvation and a life of holiness. The social activist has his, emphasizing man's social responsibility."[4]

Like other categories of Christians, sabbath saints and humanist saints generally function within closed systems. What they have incorporated into their belief system and their soul determines how they perceive what are God's will and ways. The challenge for all followers of Jesus is to affirm their personal convictions while at the same time making room for followers of Jesus who cherish convictions that are different.

INDOCTRINATED CERTAINTY

The tension for Christians who take the Bible seriously is to figure out how to handle the Bible's multimessaging. For example, "by grace you have been saved through faith," yet "we are what he has made us, created in Christ Jesus for good works, which God prepared beforehand to be our way of life" (Eph 2:8, 10). Sometimes the Scriptures speak categorically: "If you confess with your lips that Jesus is Lord and believe in your heart that God raised him from the dead, you will be saved" (Rom 10:9). Other times they speak in a reticent confessional tone: we have "the light of the knowledge of the glory of God in the face of Jesus Christ . . . in clay jars" (2 Cor 4:6-7). In this life we see "in a mirror, dimly," and know "only in part" (1 Cor 13:12).

Members of the sabbath-saints Christian fraternity tend to focus on biblical texts that are clear and definitive. They appeal to scholars who proclaim their views under the umbrellas of both systematic and biblical theology. In that way not only can doctrines be defined and defended, but God can become the exclusive property of those who affirm the Bible's objective authority. In the midst of debate they inevitably claim more and more certainty.

Those in the humanist-saints Christian fraternity gravitate toward texts that offer space for a subjective perspective. They tend more toward invitations to love than toward references to truth. Humanist saints are comfortable believing that "there is no objective laboratory (seminary, study, pulpit) where we can remove the subjective 'variables' of who we are, and where we are; rather, those very variables are essential factors in how we see God, life, ourselves, everything."[5] Over the long run, humanist saints tend to claim certainty about less and less—except for certainty about what cannot be claimed.

In reality, both sabbath saints and humanist saints should expect visits from enemies with smiling faces. Sabbath saints use the Scriptures to "overpromise" and set themselves up for disappointment. When God is expected to keep promises that were never intended, people tumble into disillusionment. Humanist saints are positioned to lapse into the other extreme. They are prone to diminish the Scriptures' power—to "underpromise." And when God is positioned so that the divine presence doesn't really matter all that much, people may eventually conclude, "Why bother?"

Evangelical scholar Vernon Grounds guides us into the middle ground: "We can and must affirm that, though blessed with divine revelation, we do not have all the answers, perhaps even many of the answers, to the problems of society. But we can and must refuse to be intimidated into irresponsible passivity by our undeniable ignorance. We can and must . . . study, discuss, reflect, think, pray and act. Yes, we can and must urge that all of us act in keeping with the insight and knowledge we now possess."[6]

CHERISHED TRUTH

A few decades ago, after I had completed my graduate work in seminary and university, I received several visits from friends and acquaintances who were in the process of giving up on God. Most of them had been brought up in families that gave much time to the weekly activities of conservative Protestant churches. These friends took me to lunch or visited for an evening and talked about why they couldn't keep their integrity and live the life of faith anymore. As they dumped their irresolvable dilemmas on me, I felt they were treating me as a "just in case" safeguard to a decision they had already made. As if I were their last stop on their way to life without God. It was unsettling to my own faith.

I pled with each of my friends in words like these: "Don't mess with the church rules and all that small stuff, or you will give it all up. Peel back the onion of faith to the center, what you cannot live without and still be a follower of Jesus. Test the essence of faith to see if it is true and if it works in the reality of your days and nights. If it is valid, it will grow; and if it isn't, it will die." I still think the counsel is solid.

Inherent in the counsel to "peel back the onion of faith" is that all aspects of truth—or sin for that matter—are not equal. Just as shoplifting is not as consequential as murder, having the truth about the mode of baptism is not as consequential as believing in the divinity and humanity of Jesus Christ. If all aspects of truth are not of equal importance in the Christian life, then discriminating between what is crucial and what is peripheral will help us guard what matters.

Here is my short list of Christian core convictions:

- God created and desires what is good.
- Christ redeemed us and the Holy Spirit energizes us.
- The Scriptures are trustworthy.
- Miracles are possible.
- God partners with people in pursuit of righteousness, love and justice.
- Involvement in communities of faith is critical.
- Accountability is certain.
- God is trustworthy and has the last word.

Cultural critic Neil Postman reminds us that "Christianity is a demanding and serious religion. When it is delivered as easy and amusing, it is another kind of religion altogether."[7] Naming what deserves to be cherished allows us to respond strategically to the central demands of the faith. Affirming a Christian core of beliefs means we have a foundation to build on and a protection from the erosion of faith.

While churches that do not cherish enough of God's revealed truth suffer from theological anorexia, other churches suffer from theological gluttony because they call for absolute levels of commitment to every aspect of their particular teaching.

VALUED PREFERENCES

Distinguishing the core of Christian truth from matters of faith that are secondary is liberating. Taking the step beyond believing that my particular Christian view of truth is the only valid Christian view to also accepting the validity of other Christian views of truth is more challenging. After all, if my views of the faith are true, how can the views of others be different from mine and be true too?

Consider the following perspectives: Accept everyone's subjectivity. Contending that anyone can completely discern God's ways and come to the Scriptures with pure objectivity is tantamount to claiming to be God. Being human has limitations. We are neither omnipotent nor omnipresent. God's wisdom is beyond our intellect. God's heart knows depths that we cannot plumb. God's vision transcends the highest reach of the world's most gifted visionaries.

The human reality is that we all walk around carrying backpacks filled with family influences, the positives and negatives of our religious upbringing, the social shaping of our cultural context, the inclinations of our temperament and the impact of our spiritual experiences with God. Not only are we earthen vessels who see through a glass darkly, but what we see is affected by the inputs that go into who we are. As John Hick succinctly points out, "To say that whatever is sincerely believed and practiced is, by definition, true, would be the end of all critical discrimination, both intellectual and moral."[8]

Distinguish *the* Christian view from *a* Christian view. When we accept our inevitable subjectivity and think reflectively on the diverse history of the Christian church, there can be no other conclusion: rather than claiming to have *the* Christian view for all God's creation, the best we can do is to embrace and be embraced by *a* Christian view as a part of God's creation. In other words, we happily distinguish between holding *the* biblical view and believing *a* biblical view. Otherwise we downsize God's family to the members of our Christian tribe who believe the same things in the same way.

Surrender either-or attitudes and embrace both-and attitudes. Acknowledging that God's family extends beyond the doctrines and rituals of "my tribe's" particular way of believing and behaving does more than make my world bigger. I am freed from viewing others with an either-or attitude and freed to embrace them with a both-and attitude. Instead of rejecting those who disagree with my particular Christian views, I am able to include others in my Christian family whether I agree with them or not.

Experiencing a both-and world has amazing results for those who have not yet lived that way. When we make room for others, they most often make room for us. And when we value the preferences of others, we discover they are remarkably open to appreciating our preferences.

DIRECTION FOR THE JOURNEY

Staying true to one's convictions while extending the right to others to affirm their convictions can be demanding. But there are proven guidelines to follow.

Confident conviction. Acknowledging everyone's subjectivity and making room for other people's Christian commitments does not require compromise of anyone's convictions. The Christian family is diverse enough to provide many places to belong. Neither should anyone be intimidated by the prevailing mood in the culture that is predisposed to validate almost any version of truth. Rather, the range of both Christian and cultural diversity is an invitation to figure out where to stand personally and how to live with confident conviction.

Author Paul Wilke articulates a vision of faith that is worthy of our confidence:

> What we seek is a belief at once transcendently compelling and eminently practical—a true, reliable, and lasting light to illuminate our lives; a spiritual force to infuse our beings and inform our

judgments; a compass by which to set our course. We want something to help us live life and confront death, a way to shape our morality, a set of principles we can take into the bedroom as well as the boardroom—a faith that can weather our various trials, moods, and seasons.[9]

Gracious orthodoxy. Confident faith generates a gracious faith, faith that resides in a sense of security that does not need to send signals of superiority, faith that accepts the inevitable ambiguity between belief beyond reasonable doubt and belief beyond a shadow of a doubt. It is faith that remains content with unanswered questions because it is grounded on Christian orthodoxy and the strength of core Christian convictions.

Evidencing a spirit of gracious orthodoxy, Kelly Brown-Douglass creatively suggests that "you should do theology like you do a crossword puzzle. First of all, you do it in pencil, because it is very arrogant to do it in pen. As you find out more, sometimes you have to change answers you thought you had. And sometimes you may never find the answer; sometimes you just have to live with the question."[10]

Spiritual humility. Religious commentator Tom Harpur reminds us that "we all walk with a limp. We're all wounded in varying degrees and ways. We're all going to fail and know weakness. It's an essential and indelible part of our humanity. . . . There are no wholly strong, perfect human beings. There are only the weak and those who pretend not to be."[11]

God walks with those who walk in spiritual humility. Faith begins only when we surrender our sense of being right. Faith continues to mature only as we stay humble enough to confess our incompleteness. Along the journey, spiritual wisdom invites us to pray, "Grant that I may seek not so much to believe as to discern."

5 Depreciating the Image of God

Those of us who drive cars and live in cities often find ourselves going around the block several times looking for a parking space. When the prospects of finding a spot get more and more remote, we are pressed to turn into parking lots that cost more than we wish to pay. Recently that was my experience in a very socially undesirable part of the city I was visiting. I pulled into a parking lot and became a little befuddled. There was no attendant in the booth, nor did I see a sign detailing how much I would have to pay for the time I was planning to stay.

After circling the block several times and not finding a better alternative, I decided to leave the car in the lot and run the risk of getting a ticket. Just as I turned off the engine, an unshaven, bedraggled man appeared before me asking, "Can I help you?"

I needed help, but he was not exactly the kind of person I was expecting to offer assistance. My first question to the man was "Do you know how much I need to pay?" He guided my attention to an obscure sign.

I did not have the six dollars in coins that I evidently needed for the machine in the corner of the lot. The man intuitively computed my dilemma and asked, "Can I get some change for you? I can go across the street and get what you need."

Although I don't like to admit it, there was a pause in my response. Glancing at the folded money in my pocket, I realized that the smallest amount I had was twenty dollars.

I looked and he looked. We looked at each other. I handed him the twenty. Then, as if reading my mind, the good Samaritan of the moment asked, "Do you trust me?"

I looked at him and, believing that the moment of dignity was more important than the money, smiled and said, "I trust you."

While my entrepreneurial new acquaintance was performing his good deed, I figured out that he really was working. He was fulfilling a self-created job description. Creatively, he was performing a function for people who needed to pay for their parking places. When he returned with bills and coins in hand, I expressed my appreciation with a generous tip. He smiled. I shook his hand and smiled too.

My theological theory has considerable space reserved for the conviction that every person on the face of the earth is created in the image of God. If we accept the creation account in Genesis, we have to conclude that there is inherent goodness in everyone (Gen 1:27). What troubles me is that my theory doesn't always show up in my behavior. Instead of instinctively giving the benefit of the doubt to people like my parking lot adviser, I assume the worst side of people's intentions.

I'm not pleading for a view of people that denies their shadow side. Sin stains human behavior. The capacity for expressing incredible evil is innate in everyone. However, I am contending that when we depreciate the image of God in people, not only do we make people less than they are, but we also become less than we are meant to be. And when that happens in our interactions with people, an enemy with a smiling face embraces us. We depreciate the image of God in people, unconsciously lower our expectations of their capacity for goodness and blind our eyes to their human beauty.

SOURCING THE GOOD
Sourcing the good in people is not the same as claiming that people are

innately good. Rather, it is asserting that people are potentially good—that they have a God-given capacity to discern and express goodness. It is also proposing that people like Adolf Hitler, Slobodan Milosevic, the Oklahoma bomber Timothy McVeigh and the terrorist Osama Bin Laden are not human norms. They are despicable, depraved exceptions to the norm.

Theologians have been playing off the good and evil dimensions of human beings for centuries. The challenge has been to affirm what is noble and beautiful in the world while at the same time acknowledging the human capacity for sin and corruption. The godly gift of *common grace* has been the main theological descriptor of the human potential to pursue good and do what's right. Advocates of a creation-centered spirituality believe that the retained image of God in humanity makes it possible for people to reach their spiritual potential. The designations *original sin* and *human depravity* are used to indicate the inherent inclination of people to choose evil over good and chase after darkness rather than light.

The practical question that faces us is, when we observe people doing good, what is the explanation for the good and what is the source of their goodness? The easy answer is God. The Creator God is behind human acts of kindness and expressions of virtuous behavior. When a neighbor spontaneously shovels the snow off our driveway, when without complaint or expectation coworkers cover for us when we are sick, or when a stranger stops on a busy highway to help change a flat tire, they are giving evidence that traces of the image of God reside in them. On those occasions when politicians pay a personal price to pass unpopular but far-sighted social legislation, or when decision-makers in the United Nations sign international accords to protect the rights of children, God is at work through those people. When business people forced to declare formal bankruptcy still work long and hard to pay off creditors when legally they do not have to do so, we have the opportunity to propose a toast to both God and the goodness of principled people.

Cynics will argue that neighbors and coworkers are really motivated by self-interest, expecting us to return the favors, and that politicians, civil servants and businesspeople are all driven by ulterior motives. Admittedly, arguing for pure motives is difficult. However, the human capacity to observe and celebrate the human ability to do good is an argument for the existence of virtue in the human spirit. Gandhi rightly believed, "He who does not see God in the next person he meets, need look no further." Confucius remarked, "Everything has its beauty, but not everyone sees it."

Author Samuel Miller's perspective assumes God's presence in creation: "In the muddled mess of this world, in the confusion and the boredom, we ought to be able to spot something—an event, a person, a memory, an act, a turning of the soul, a flash of bright wings, the surprise of sweet compassion—somewhere we ought to pick out a glory to celebrate."[1]

ACCENTUATING THE BAD

Many Christian people are vulnerable to believing the worst about human nature. They emphasize our inevitable sinfulness and the disregard for God's will and ways that underscores our capacity for brokenness and corruption. The obvious problem of sin, the centrality of John 3:16 in the Scriptures, the dominant influence of Reformed theology and the death of Christ on the cross converge in our thinking. Without repentance and confession, people everywhere are on their way to a hell on earth in the present tense and hell after death in the eternal sense. There is another factor in the equation. Churches that emphasize Christ's death on the cross while neglecting the redeeming consequences of being created in the image of God accentuate the tendency to believe the worst.

Balance is a beautiful thing when it comes to how we conceive of God. On the one hand, when we overplay the importance of Christ as Redeemer, we run the risk of overplaying the human capacity for sin and evil. On the other hand, affirming God's image in us and the built-in goodness that lets righteousness rule tends to overemphasize our human potential. The beautiful balance is to be both creation-centered and cross-centered. It is to take the creation account seriously and stand tall in the image of God. It is also to bow to the purpose of the cross and with contriteness confess that without Christ's intervention we are spiritually destitute.

Inevitably, how we think about God informs how we think about ourselves. If we are oriented to God as Creator, it will be easier to look at ourselves in the mirror and say, "I like what I see. God's beauty marks are a part of who I am." If we are oriented to Christ as Redeemer, the mirror will more likely reveal our fallenness and sin. Instead of beauty marks we will see scars and feel shame.

DAMAGING STEREOTYPES

The image of God appears to be depreciated in some people groups more than others. We may struggle to believe that God's image has equal status in criminals and prostitutes, or in people who are extremely obese or physically maimed. We may be blinded to God's beauty marks in the chronically unemployed and in those who are members of minority groups. Another group that suffers from negative stereotyping is the severely disabled.

Jean Vanier, the founder of the L'Arche movement, which has over one hundred communities for the intellectually disabled in nineteen countries, contends that "people with disabilities are devalued in this world." Vanier's experience has taught him that they have much to teach us. "When I give baths to people with severe disabilities, I have to be tender. I have to be very sensitive to each movement—it is being sensitive not to ideas but to a person in their physical reality. I mean the way they hug you. There is mystery in the tenderness. So they have brought me from the world of ideas, the world of power, into the primary world of the relationship."[2]

The beauty of the image of God in people can catch us off guard. Friends of our family have a twelve-year-old daughter named Jennifer who lives with Down syndrome. When Jennifer was preparing for her baptism, the interviewing deacon asked her, "What do you like about God?" Jennifer smiled and said, "God is handsome. God is good. And God loves me." Jennifer's concept of God is a gift to enrich all of us.

Minority groups have suffered from damaging stereotypes, and consequently God's image in them has been demeaned. At the beginning of the twentieth century, an age when blacks were heavily discriminated against and segregated, Carrie Best lived in Nova Scotia and was the province's first black publisher. She was an outspoken advocate for racial equality, and her life was about service to others. She didn't care about recognition; she was anxious to work for truth and justice.

For years the Roseland Theatre had seated black and white patrons together. But in December 1941 the owner changed the seating policy and relegated blacks to the balcony.

After hearing that a group of black high school girls had been told to leave their main floor seats, Ms. Best wrote to the theater owner: "I am a citizen and taxpayer and have the right to sit where I wish in any public place. As I am too tired to come to the theatre tonight, I respectfully request you, Sir, to instruct your employees to sell me the ticket I wish when next I come to the theatre."

When she and her son showed up as promised, they sat downstairs and refused to budge until a police officer showed up. Best hired a lawyer and sued. After a one-day trial, the all-white jury sided with the theater and the judge awarded costs against Best. Not only had she lost, but she also owed the Roseland Theatre $156.07.

Carrie Best suffered a legal and financial loss, but her affirmation still rings true: "I am a person, born in the image of God. I have intelligence. I am honest. And I am as good, if not better than anybody who walks the face of this earth."[3]

Eugene Rivers is a modern day African American who raises his voice for the cause of racial equality, pointing out what gets unconsciously rooted in a culture. "Angel food cake is white; devil's food cake is chocolate. Good guys wear white cowboy hats; bad boys wear the black hats. There are black lies and there are white lies. There is black magic and there is white magic. There is an entire constellation of symbols and images that permeate every dimension of our thinking."[4] Over the long term, these embedded images have taken a terrible toll: "You teach a people to hate themselves for 386 years, calling them everything but a child of God, and you don't have to pull the trigger. If you program that child for so long to see himself a certain way, he'll self-destruct. This isn't rocket science."[5]

Stereotypes damage and demean. Our cultures have made significant social strides toward racial equality. Access to jobs and executive ranks, opportunities in the arts and the media, and cultural respect for the contributions of African Americans continue to rise. Still, our hands are not clean, and unarticulated attitudes of superiority continue to work subtle harm. We would do well to get down on our knees and pray.

MORAL INTENTIONS

Why do we act the way we do? Why are we prone to judge the actions of others? Why do we extend our moral expectations beyond the members of our families and people we know by name?

In a crosscultural study, *The Moral Sense,* James Q. Wilson contends that "people necessarily make moral judgments . . . and that we will get a lot further in understanding how we live as a species if we recognize that we are bound together by mutual interdependence and a common moral sense."[6] Wilson goes on to assert that people are morally predisposed to express the virtues of sympathy, fairness, self-control and duty.

We have all felt *sympathy.* In varying degrees, the trials and joys of others affect us. Children share the distress of a crying baby who is sick. Reports of earthquakes and the loss of life and shelter trigger inward groans in us. Whenever I hear of an untimely death, there is a lament in my spirit. We blink back tears of joy as our favorite Olympic athlete ascends the podium to receive a gold medal as our national anthem is played. Our capacity to empathize and sympathize with people is part of our moral sense.

The virtue of *fairness* is another dimension of our built-in morality. "That's not fair" is often the first moral judgment uttered by a child.[7] The family practice of one sibling's cutting the last piece of a cake into two pieces and then giving the second sibling the right to choose first illustrates how fairness is expressed and taught. We seem to be wired to a frequency of fairness. When a long-term, close-to-retirement employee is fired without cause, we know "that's not fair." When we've been standing in a slow grocery checkout line and a new line is opened that allows the person who came last to be first, we have the same "not fair" feeling. It's part of our moral sense.

We develop sets of social habits. We are subject to the shaping influence of our family, friends, faith, geography and socioeconomic circumstances and the diverse dynamics of our culture. Still, I contend that the regard we have for people who evidence a healthy measure of *self-control* is a reflection of our shared human morality.

Without self-control, our life together would be social chaos. Timetables would be irrelevant. We would work only when we felt like it. Public morality would be reduced to personal preferences. Sexual permissiveness would defy any shared definition. Life would be like driving on busy streets without any traffic laws. Rules, rituals and social etiquette would disappear. Anarchy would reign.

An absence of self-control would also throw our personal life into disarray. We would eat only what we wanted, our addictions would multiply, mothers would be more concerned about their personal schedule than nursing their baby, students wouldn't study, children would lose their reference points for growing up. Life would be subject to the rule of impulse. It is no wonder that one of the fruits of the Spirit is self-control. Surely God is sending us a signal: What is already built into our human capacity needs to be refined and enabled.

Why are people willing to honor obligations in the absence of social and personal rewards for doing so? Carpenters sleep better at night when the beams and joists they have put in place are constructed properly. We prefer to live within the law even when our chance of being caught and punished is minimal. We pay our taxes not to escape an audit but mostly to do what's right and fulfill our civic *duty*. We know that a single vote in an election doesn't matter that much, but we still make the effort to vote. We make charitable contributions with a modest tax benefit, yes, but without any further recognition beyond an impersonal printed receipt. A sense of duty is part of the human disposition to honor an array of obligations with no hope of reward or fear of punishment.[8]

Those who do not acknowledge God as Creator often look for other explanations, but the best explanation for the sense of moral oughtness in human beings is that God is the source. Certainly the human conscience is subject to social shaping and interpersonal formation, but the capacity to develop a conscience in the first place is more evidence that the image of God is planted in the human spirit.

DIRECTION FOR THE JOURNEY

Calculating the image of God into our view of ourselves and each other is a gift of creation. The Creator's image in us affirms the God-given goodness that is rooted in our humanity. Accordingly, God invites me to see the goodness in you. Instead of being biased to expect the worst, we are invited to see the goodness in each other. And because we are pointed in the direction of virtue, we can look at others with the eyes of a discoverer. We can discover God's goodness in each other.

We know that God's goodness in us commingles with our sin and self-interest. Even with Christ's forgiving presence in us, our capacity for evil remains. Our readiness to reject what we know to be right and choose what we know to be wrong persists.

My educator friend Carla Nelson is fond of saying, "The Christian life is a progressive restoration of a lost likeness."[9] Beyond radical divine interventions at particular times, we will need Christ's continual touch-up as long as we keep on the journey. So we play and work, relate and interact with the people God brings into our lives, praying, "Grant that I may seek not so much to believe as to discern."

PART 2

WORLDLY ENEMIES
WITH SMILING FACES

*Grant that I may seek not so much
to be understood as to understand.*

The world can be a dangerous place. People who choose to construct their life without regard for God are particularly vulnerable. They are making a severe miscalculation: they believe they can make it on their own.

Regrettably, those who believe God is unnecessary will inevitably become less than they desire to be. They will not have eyes to see divine wisdom. They will not have ears to hear godly counsel. They will hunger for meaning and not be satisfied. People who leave God out of the equation of their life may never figure this out, but they are destined to fall short of the vision they have for their well-being.

Making a commitment to God's ways does not come with a guarantee that we will maximize our potential and become all we desire to be. It can still be hard to discern divine wisdom and act on godly counsel. Even with God's direction and enabling, we aspire to figure life out, but our fallenness keeps us from getting it all right. For one thing, we are subject to the world's influence. The spirit of the age embraces us, and we return the embrace.

This section names worldly enemies with smiling faces and aims to critique contemporary culture without condemning it. The intent is to nurture a compassionate understanding of people who live with the assumption that God is unnecessary. We want to develop the godly wisdom of St. Francis, seeking not so much to be understood as to understand.

6   Self-Construction

Every time I hear someone labeling people as "believers" and "unbelievers," I wince. If a Christian makes the statement, I know what they mean. They are simply sorting people. One group is people who profess to be followers of Jesus; the other group is people who make no claim to be Christian believers.

The reason I wince is that I'm convinced there are no unbelievers. Everyone believes something. If you breathe, you believe. Admittedly, not everyone can clearly describe what they have concluded about life. However, when we listen, our daily interaction with people reveals their views about issues, their values, their beliefs about right and wrong. Even when beliefs are disconnected from formal systems or orthodox creeds, they still exist in people's self-design. Whether they consciously perceive it or not, people who do not frame their life with Christian beliefs use other construction materials to build it.

EVERYONE BUILDS

We live in times that encourage self-construction. The spirit of the age invites us to design ourselves. We are expected to parade our personal preferences and become our own authority. The underlying goal is to be autonomous in as many categories of life as possible.

This does not mean people get up in the morning and say, "I want to give myself to something shallow. I think I'll expend my energy on stuff that in the end doesn't matter." Still, people who choose to construct their life without God are setting out on a dangerous journey.

The danger lurks in the potential to actually achieve a self-constructed autonomy. No matter how wealthy, successful, privileged and powerful people may become, self-construction is an enemy with a smiling face. Whatever level of social status one may reach, life without God will always be less than it is meant to be. Regardless of achievements reached or awards received, people who are disconnected from God will not reach their full potential. Their life may even be marked by principled decisions and humanitarian concern, but they will be incomplete. It is impossible to be self-constructed and still be fully satisfied with oneself. God designed us for more.

JESUS' LESSONS ON LIVING

The Sermon on the Mount includes a short story that gives direction on how to build our life.

> Everyone then who hears these words of mine and acts on them will be like a wise man who built his house on rock. The rain fell, the floods came, and the winds blew and beat on that house, but it did not fall, because it had been founded on rock. And everyone who hears these words of mine and does not act on them will be like a foolish man who built his house on sand. The rain fell, and the floods came, and the winds blew and beat against that house, and it fell—and great was its fall! (Mt 7:24-28)

Jesus' teaching can be outlined succinctly:

Everyone builds their life on something:

- Wise people, God-focused people, build on rock.
- Unwise people, God-ignoring people, build on sand.

Everyone also faces storms.

- Life beats up on the wise and the unwise, the God-focused and the God-ignoring people.

However, some building materials are better than others.

- In the end, wise builders cope with storms better than unwise builders. The God-focused people handle the storms better than the God-ignoring people.

Jesus' underlying message is that there are significant differences between God-focused people and God-ignoring people. God-ignoring people are restricted to the limits of their inner resources. Of necessity, people who have little regard for God become inward-looking people. They are left with the challenge of building their life out of materials housed within their human capacity.

The good news for God-ignoring people is that God has created human beings with potential for incredible capacities. The ability to think and problem solve, the capacity to distinguish between right and wrong, sensitivity to experience emotion and discern life from another person's point of view, creativity and ingenuity, the ability to learn from mistakes, interpersonal skills—all these capacities have resulted in the construction of some very impressive God-ignoring people.

Admittedly, not everyone is born with the same skills or equal opportunity to develop to their full moral and emotional potential. The wounds life inflicts often turn people's good intentions into drives to get even. The discipline to choose right over wrong again and again cannot come easily for God-ignoring people. In the long run self-made people usually end up worshiping themselves, the people who matter to them and the goals that inspire them. Regrettably, they often become slaves to their own drive for self-fulfillment.

God-focused people come to the demands of life with the same range of human capacities as God-ignoring people. However, there is an enormous difference. While God-ignoring people live within the limits of their human capacities, God-focused people look out beyond themselves. They look to God. They count on direction from the Scriptures and expect the Holy Spirit to counsel and energize their human spirit.

God's presence becomes a resource for living according to God's design. God is an enabler. God's presence enables people to choose good and walk away from evil. God's Spirit gives people the ability to discern what is right and best, instills attitudes that soften harsh judgments, and increases their capacity to behave in Christlike ways. God's presence lifts the level of the human will to make right choices that perhaps would not be made otherwise. God is a positive element in people's lives, whether they are celebrating or suffering. God's presence allows people to encounter life as it is meant to be experienced and shared with others.

God-focused people distinguish themselves from God-ignoring people at another critical point. God's truth serves as a map for negotiating the intersections on the journey. I'm not saying that reading God's truth map is easy or automatic. However, people who seek to discern God's truth and obey it live with an astonishing advantage. Instead of looking only inside for direction, they look outside to God's revealed wisdom. Whether the question has to do with values, ethics, relationships, sex, money, political theory or social justice, God-focused people have the inside track on finding direction for living right.

The difficulty with Christian theory is that it doesn't always translate into reality. Too often followers of Jesus miss the mark of their good intentions. Past pain and wounds along the way can drain the capacity to be obedient. Morning prayers of commitment to build life on Jesus' teachings are overruled by afternoon decisions that disregard God. Far too frequently, sinful practices transition from "I won't do it again" to rationalizations that make doing it again acceptable. It is only God's interventions of grace and promptings to begin again that get God-focused people back on track. Still, God-focused people live in God's presence and are drawn toward seeking the truth at every turn.

Whether we are God-ignoring people or God-focused people, cultural commentator Jean Bethke Elshtain captures what we all feel: "In the deep of night, with the clock ticking and sleepless anxiety rising, our current version of the American dream must be having second thoughts. Why? We don't want anyone to hamper us. But we do think there's too much . . . plain old-fashioned raw selfishness, out there."[1]

EVERYONE FACES STORMS

A central message in Jesus' rock and sand parable is that God-focused people who keep their attention on God's ways avoid a lot of storms. In contrast, God-ignoring people can easily create life storms.

Some storms are part of huge systems that wreak havoc on everyone everywhere. Other storms are self-generated, the consequences of intention and choice. In any case, whether we build with God or without God, there is no way to escape points of pain. One of life's guarantees is that we will all face storms. Stormy times and suffering are inevitable for everyone.

People who get caught in the path of a hurricane or in the twisting power of a tornado are subject to forces stronger than they are. When there is a traffic accident, when lab reports confirm cancer, when a young mother or father suffers a fatal heart attack, people feel as if they have been hit by a stray bomb.

Billions of people live under systemic conditions that keep them bound in poverty. These people live in a continual storm: there is no access to education or adequate health care, and jobs are scarce. They didn't create their situation. They were just born into the storm of poverty.

Too frequently in our battered world the lives of the innocent are devastated by war. I remember standing on the tarmac at a military base as part of a team welcoming refugees from Kosovo. As the refugees waited for clearance, I thought they looked just like those of us who were there to greet them. But there was sadness in their spirits. No one was laughing. One woman in a late stage of pregnancy moved through the line with three young children. Would she ever see her husband again? Was he already dead? When the military sent out a truck to unload the luggage of the 262 passengers, it came back with a total of 42 items, most of them canvas duffle bags. Not one of those refugees was there because they wanted to be there. They just got caught in a fierce storm.

Other types of storms are self-induced, the consequences of bad choices or addictive behaviors. Those who harbor grudges or refuse to forgive people who have wronged them invite turbulence in their life.

Spouses who betray their marriage covenant for moments of sexual pleasure with someone else produce ominous storm clouds. People stir up recipes for storms when they surrender to anger, hate or selfishness.

God-ignoring people who get caught contravening the laws of life that are etched into creation are especially vulnerable to generating self-designed storms. Their commitment to self-construction leaves them without God's wisdom and protection. Their drive to be autonomous exposes them to life's howling winds and raging rains. Without intending to do so, self-constructed, God-ignoring people are forced to cope with enemies with smiling faces. They think they have all the resources they need to make it on their own. In the end, that calculation is disastrous.

ALL BUILDING MATERIALS ARE NOT EQUAL

The Christian appeal to all people who live on this side of heaven is "Build your life on rock." Embrace Jesus and his teachings, pursue the will and ways of God the Father, draw energy from the personal presence of the Spirit. And when the storms come, expect to still be standing after the disorder has dissipated and passed on.

The alternative in Jesus' parable to building one's life on rock is to build on sand. It is to self-construct by first drawing energy and insight from one's inner being. Self-construction counts on the capacities of human ingenuity and the ability to piece together life along the way. There is a dependence on the will to make preferred choices and the conscience to discern what is good, better and best. Thoughtful people who build their lives out of sand pick their way carefully through vocational decisions, moral dilemmas and relationships. Sometimes the ways of the world rule their choices, on other occasions it is family history that provides direction. The sources of influence vary, but one matter is constant. Self-constructed people have the final word on the materials they use to weave the fabric of their life. Whatever materials those may be, they are inferior when compared to the rock of the Christian faith. People who build without God run the risk of collapsing under the storms that will undoubtedly invade their lives.

Technical theologians and biblical purists may not applaud my interpretation that follows. But a review of reality among God-focused people and God-ignoring people reveals that *both* groups tend to build their lives on a mixture of rock and sand. God-focused people will have more rock than sand, and God-ignoring people will most often have more sand than rock. There is one further critical distinction. Christ's presence with God-focused people is like cement holding the pieces of rock and sand together. Rock and sand without cement leave life spread in disarray. The presence of cement opens the possibility of fusing life in a cohesive whole. The Christian advantage emerges again. And the reason for the advantage is clear: some building materials are better than others.

We all take risks with the materials we use to build our lives. People who say no to Christ's claims must find other ways to cement themselves. Mike, for example, hinged his life hopes on the ambition of becoming a pilot for a commercial airline. And he accomplished what he set out to achieve. During his twenties and thirties, Mike soared. He married the love of his life; they started a family and bought their first house. His dreams were all coming true. Then, during his thirty-seventh year, Mike had a severe heart attack. Although disability insurance allowed him to keep paying the mortgage, he was never able to sit at the controls of another plane. Mike never really recovered from this devastation. The family survived the trauma, but afterward there was always more anger than laughter, more resentment than contentment. Mike risked his life on his vocation, and when he lost it he crumpled into permanent despair.

Recently I was traveling with two World Vision colleagues. We had spent the day together, and a few minutes before I was to leave, James said in his rather quiet voice, "Don, I doubt that you know that three months ago I lost my wife. We were traveling in a small bus that had an accident. At first it appeared that her only injury was a broken arm. However, after coming home from the hospital she developed complications, and before the problem could be determined, she died."

I gasped. After attempting to express my sympathy, I asked, "How old was your wife, and what are the ages of your children?"

Pushing back his tears, James softly answered, "My wife was thirty-two, my son is four, and my daughter is two."

We talked about the challenges James was facing. How was it possible to maintain his job that demanded travel and still care for his little ones? We probed his pain and lamented his loss.

In the midst of our exchange our colleague Daniel spoke up. "What has amazed us is James's capacity to cope. God has given him incredible strength. The pain is deep and still hurts, but James is making his way. We are walking with him, and God is with him."

We prayed together, and as I said goodbye and walked away, I thought with gratitude, *Some building materials are better than others.*

SACREDNESS OF CHOICE

The most compelling cultural force in North America feeding the hunger for autonomy is the assumption that we have the right to make choices. Whether we are purchasing breakfast cereal, shopping for an automobile, making a lifestyle decision, choosing our preferred family form or offering a viewpoint on euthanasia, we assume that we have the prerogative to decide. Modern culture has deified choice.

Missiologist Lesslie Newbigin observes, "Fundamental to our modern Western culture [is] the fact that it has enormously enlarged the area in which the individual is free to make his own choices. A vast amount of what earlier ages and other cultures simply accepted as given facts of life are now subject to human decision."[2]

The range of choices available to us is enormous. Not long ago I was visiting a small city on the East Coast. It was Sunday morning, and I decided to attend a worship service. On the way out of the hotel, I walked by a large window that provided a view of an adjacent casino. I looked at my watch; it was 10:45 a.m. I looked up again and watched people put money in slot machines and pull down the handles. The moment presented a symbol of choice: to church or to the casino?

Life is like walking into a music store with a vast selection of CDs and tapes. Competing voices cry out, "Listen to me, buy me, try me, experience me." The parade of choices seems endless. Do I embrace the virtues of Mother Teresa or the exploits of Madonna? Should I opt for the cultural standard of "Love yourself first" or the biblical standard of "Love your neighbor as yourself"? Church consultant Mike Regele commends, "People today choose the construction of reality they find most appealing. They look for the form of story that provides the greatest meaning for them. For many this is an interactive process of embracing one new reality after another."[3]

One choice is ultimate: Do I retain my autonomy or surrender myself to the God of creation and Christ of redemption? Do I give up my commitment to self-control, or do I walk toward Jesus and say yes to his embrace? People who self-construct choose to keep God out of their world. In Phillip Johnson's apt description, every self-constructed "human becomes a 'godlet'—with as much authority to set standards as any other godlet or combination of godlets."[4]

Sociologist Reginald Bibby offers good counsel to all "godlets" who are ruled by their personal viewpoints: "Precisely because we encourage choices, we need to champion the critical concept of discernment. People need to learn how to choose."[5]

SECULARIZATION SEDUCES

In the words of psychiatrist Robert Coles, "God awaits us, as do the various houses of worship that insist upon and celebrate the primacy of the sacred, yet we yield to or seek outright the profane: ideas and values and habits and interests that have their origin in our earthly lives, our day-to-day desires, worries, frustrations, resentments."[6]

In the Western world we seek to be discerning and make our choices within societies that are becoming more and more secular. Whatever our mix of rock and sand may be, whether we are God-focused or God-ignoring people, we are subject to the seduction of secularism. This subtle appeal is to misplace our worship. Even if we attend church regularly, our aspirations risk being diverted from the works of righteousness to the pursuits of self-construction.

Whether we are serious followers of Jesus or people who mostly self-construct, I suspect the temptation to give in to secularism, to live as if we had no real need for God, never goes away. Teenagers live with a sense of invincibility, which makes God optional at best. People in their

twenties and thirties are so vocationally and family pressured that reserv-
ing room for God requires enormous effort. In our forties and fifties, if
life has been kind to us we have pretty much figured out how to make
life work on our terms. Then in our sixties the demands of planning for
retirement and the opportunity to do things we've not had time for make
us vulnerable to yet another expression of self-construction.

DIRECTION FOR THE JOURNEY

Writer Anne Lamott invites us to turn away from the secular appeal of
self-construction and find life with spiritual purpose. "Most of the people I know who have what I want—which is to say, purpose, heart, balance, gratitude, joy—are people with a deep sense of spirituality. . . .
They follow a brighter light than the glimmer of their own candle." [7]

God-focused people follow a Light much brighter than their own.
God-ignoring people are left with the glimmer of their own candle. C. S.
Lewis articulates the difference—and the consequences: "There are only
two kinds of people in the end: those who say to God, 'Thy will be done,'
and those to whom God says, in the end, 'Thy will be done.'"[8]

Along the way and in the end, I want to be among those who welcome
God with "Thy will be done." And in whatever measure I share life with
those to whom God says, "Thy will be done," my prayer is "Grant that I
may seek not so much to be understood as to understand."

7   Affluenza

The MasterCard television advertisement is so creative it merits applause. The images awaken desires of various kinds: errant golf shots on a stunning course with friends laughing, travel to exotic places, dream dates, intimate times with family members. Then you hear the words, "There are some things money can't buy . . . for everything else there is MasterCard." In other words, the "make you happy" experiences you can't buy cost lots of money, so hurry up and lay down the card.

MONEY MATTERS

Money is like a knife, amoral in itself. The moral virtue or vice lies in how you use it. You can peel a potato, slice your finger, carve a wooden statue or stab someone in the back. The Scriptures present the same neutral view of money. It is not money that is immoral or evil; the *love* of money is what creates the moral issue. "The love of money is a root of all kinds of evil, and in their eagerness to be rich some have wandered away from the faith and pierced themselves with many pains" (1 Tim 6:10). Eagerness to be rich can turn people away from God and into paths of self-inflicted pain. When that happens, when the "almighty" dollar becomes too important, money is an enemy with a smiling face.

The power of money for good and for evil is a well-established fact of life. On the good side of the ledger, money is a resource to be used to meet personal and social needs. Money provides shelter, feeds families and makes education and healthcare accessible. Money is the medium of exchange of goods and services of an interdependent economy. It is a critical means to the end of our collective well-being.

Paychecks are the fruit of honest work that give people the capacity to meet their commitments and live with dignity. Money is a fabulous resource to share with people who are struggling, to send "I believe in you" messages and gifts that say "I love you." Money can be used for wonderful parties and celebrations, the memories of which last for years.

On the dark side of the equation, an insatiable drive for money can motivate the most despicable behavior imaginable. The uncontrolled pursuit of money generates greed, fraud, exploitation, crime and inordinate selfishness. To get their hands on more money, sons and daughters will betray their mothers and fathers. Employers abuse the people who work for them, and whether they are abused or not, employees steal from their companies. Vulnerable lovers are romanced and swindled. Corrupt presidents and prime ministers abuse the people they claim to be serving to fill their own treasure chests. People are prepared to kill and to die for money.

CONSUMER CULTURE

North American culture attempts to control the conduct of potential consumers. The department store with the longest history in Canada, the Hudson's Bay Company, markets under the advertising slogan "Shopping is good." The slogan reinforces the premise that consumption is a social duty. How else can one be a responsible citizen in a materialistic society?

In our consumer culture, the options that bring comfort and convenience a little closer to our reach will have the marketing edge. Outside North America, the city of Geneva, Switzerland, sets the standard for consumer cities. Set in the shadow of the Alps, it is designed with meticulous care. Walking the streets, you feel as if the whole city is a Swiss clock that keeps precise time. The crowded streets are tidy and pristine.

Even the cars are washed and shiny. Panhandling is rare, and there is very little evidence of poverty. Except for the awkward presence of Mc-Donald's, specialized stores are the norm. Swiss watches and knives, music boxes and specialty chocolate lead the consumer parade. Geneva is a place where quality reigns and less than the best offends.

As I walked those streets I wondered, *If you live in Geneva, how long can you hold out before you are convinced you are living an inferior life unless you have decadent chocolate in the cupboard, elaborate watches for work, casual and special social occasions, an array of knives for every purpose and music boxes adorning your shelves?* But then another series of questions invaded my mind: *How much chocolate can you eat? How many watches can you wear? How many Swiss knives can you use? How many music boxes can you possess before they become clutter?*

The Geneva syndrome is present in every city and community in North America. As Neil Postman has observed, once the "god of consumerism" takes over, the basic moral axiom becomes "Whoever dies with the most toys wins."[1]

MONEY MUSINGS

There are two dimensions of money and materialism that continue to mystify me: Why don't the broken promises of materialism dampen the drive to accumulate more? And why is enough never enough?

When I feed my physical thirst with a tall glass of water or a strong cup of coffee, I don't feel thirsty anymore. Physiologically I am altered; my thirst is quenched. While I do get thirsty again, once I get a drink I readily reach a level of satisfaction that takes away my craving for more. However, when I feed my hunger for materialistic stuff, whatever I acquire neither changes me nor shuts down my wish for more. The television set with the flatter screen and sharper image that promises to improve the quality of my life leaves me unchanged. The acquisition of a newer car that I was told would enhance my self-image results in my feeling exactly the same about me. What puzzles me is that even though I know that having more will not really alter my quality of life, I am still open to the possibility of increasing my possessions.

Once I had lunch with a wealthy and very generous man. He was a building contractor with a long history of buying large tracts of vacant land and turning them into housing developments. In the midst of a candid conversation about money, he suddenly admitted that "enough never seems to be enough." Without any sense of superiority, he mused, "It's common knowledge that I am worth millions of dollars. You also know my commitment to support various ministries in significant ways. Still, I'm never quite satisfied with what is on the ledger. Why not a few more million? Enough never seems to be enough."

Why are our bank accounts never full? Why do we keep going back to the stores for more? Is it the consequence of being exposed daily to hundreds of advertising images? What part does one's family history play in instilling a sense of financial security or insecurity? Does the materialistic spirit of the age massage our mind into believing that all is not well unless we do well financially?

Author David Hilfiker's assessment is part of the answer. "Some fundamental set of societal values has shifted, co-opting the ways in which we think. Today, we have trouble understanding service, sharing, justice, and equality, not because we are worse people than 40 years ago, but because, over the last generation, we've unwittingly transformed capitalism into a religion."[2]

Whatever the answers may be, money matters. And if we don't get control of the power of money in our life, it will get control of us. We will end up wrestling with a highly influential enemy with a smiling face.

SPIRITUAL WARNINGS

If capitalism is the culture's religion, then shopping is a spiritual experience for its citizens. "Shopping malls are our modern cathedrals of consumption. It used to be the church where you saw fellow community members. Now it's the mall. The parking lots are filled. There's an almost sacred quality given to the act of consuming. There's a certain standardized feeling in the malls, just like the old cathedrals of yore."[3]

Jesus understood the power of money and the dangers of malls. His candid warning to his disciples still stands:

"Truly I tell you, it will be hard for a rich person to enter the kingdom of heaven. Again I tell you, it is easier for a camel to go through the eye of a needle than for someone who is rich to enter the kingdom of God." When the disciples heard this, they were greatly astounded and said, "Then who can be saved?" But Jesus looked at them and said, "For mortals it is impossible, but for God all things are possible." (Mt 19:23-26)

Jesus' visual hyperbole of a camel struggling to crawl through a narrow, low gate in the walls of Old Jerusalem ("the eye of the needle") confirms what we know experientially. The daily and lifelong dynamics of acquiring and spending money are threatening to our spiritual well-being. Without God's intervention, we are headed for trouble.

There is another spiritually related money matter that deserves attention. Living as obedient and faithful followers of Jesus often increases people's bank balances. They become more responsible with their money. Disciplined patterns in the workplace often generate increased income for faithful people. They are also less apt to waste money on bad habits. The history of churches that begin working with poor people is that those people move up the social and economic ladder. You only need to drive by a few church parking lots today to realize that one of the byproducts of the faith is increased financial stability.

The advice of John Wesley to upwardly mobile Methodists more than two centuries ago is a pointed reminder of the dilemma of our own success:

I fear, wherever riches have increased, the essence of religion has decreased in the same proportion. Therefore I do not see how it is possible, in the nature of things, for any revival of religion to continue long. For religion must necessarily produce both industry and frugality, and these cannot but produce riches. But as riches increase, so will pride, anger, and love of the world in all its branches.[4]

How can we cope? On the one hand, although Jesus was fully aware of the power and dangers of riches, only once did he command, "Go, sell your possessions" (Mt 19:21). On the other hand, Jesus says to us all, "No one can serve two masters; for a slave will either hate the one and love the other, or be devoted to the one and despise the other. You cannot serve God and wealth" (Mt 6:24).

The challenge is to control the power of money over us. Being aware that the most creative people on the planet are fine-tuning advertising's cunning influence is a start. Recognizing that we are being seduced to become disciples of our consumer culture and enticed to bless material affluence as the lord of life will allow us to erect walls of resistance. To believe that "for God all things are possible" will be our salvation.

BEWARE OF AFFLUENZA

The gods of affluence pervade our materialistic world without the sound of sirens. The economic traffic of the culture just keeps moving along. We work, we worship, we spend and we accumulate. Interest rates ebb and flow, and unless a recession overstays its welcome, for those of us who have the privilege of being employed, life just keeps rolling along. But when we pause and reflect, there are warning signs. There are indicators that the disease of "affluenza" is taking up residence and spreading its fever.

Wealth without meaning. Wealth and comfort are a lot like Novocain: they numb us. And when the accumulation of wealth becomes the ultimate reason for living, it blocks out other concerns. In pursuit of more and more, relationships can be sacrificed, time is misdirected, and once-cherished principles are abandoned. Rather than being a means toward noble ends, money and its privileges become ends in themselves. Certainly there are pleasures along the way, but the price is inordinate. Instead of fulfilling God-ordained purposes for life and love, there is activity without meaning and achievement without fulfillment. Cultural analyst Douglas Coupland sums up the result: "The accumulation of material goods is at an all-time high, but so is the number of people who feel emptiness in their lives."[5]

The acquisition of wealth for wealth's sake only proves that we are designed for more than accumulating and consuming.

Power without responsibility. Decision-makers in democratic cultures like to talk about being equal, about being "egalitarian." Equal rights and equal access are certainly preferable to inequality. But in practical affairs of living and working, equality is a myth. People with position and wealth wield power. And unless the power people link their positions to intentional social responsibility, the gap between equality and inequality widens.

According to long-time social advocate Ron Sider, "today the average CEO earns in two hours what the person working at the minimum wage earns in a full year of work."[6] Free enterprise has always rewarded those deemed responsible for making more and more money. Presidents get paid more than vice presidents. Senior pastors get paid more than associate pastors. While economic gain is seldom given complete free rein, moral considerations to restrain economic gain is hard to sell to both church elders and stock-laden boards of directors.

I have no wish to dismiss egalitarian intentions or to demean the importance of executives showing profit or pastors claiming increased attendance on annual reports. But executives and others who have power need to realize that they have special vulnerability. To them I would say: Beware of using your power without heed to those who have no choice but to live with the consequences of your power. Surrender to a self-inventory. Active concern for fairness and justice will be an indication that you are pursuing a responsible future. Indifference and lack of awareness will be signs that the infection of affluenza has struck.

Leisure without liberty. Leisure is one of the good gifts of affluence. G. K. Chesterton, the notable British Catholic writer, reflects on the various types of activities that get lumped under the rubric of leisure: "I think the name of leisure has come to cover three totally different things. The first is being allowed to do something. The second is being allowed to do anything. And the third, perhaps the most rare and precious, is being allowed to do nothing."[7] Who in their right mind would not welcome the choice of all three types?

The full enjoyment of leisure, however, is not guaranteed for those who can afford the luxury. Enjoying one's leisure is an art. And affluenza interferes with the practice of this art.

It's a sign when our last thought before we go to sleep and our first thought when we wake up is about interest rates and investments. Compulsively checking the value of one's stock portfolio on the Internet is a symptom of the fever of affluenza. Walking in the neighborhood or down the tenth fairway with money matters on one's mind means that money has exceeded its real value. Having lunch with friends and wondering about their net worth is an indication that one's leisure has lost its liberty. Affluenza is evident when money-related matters are too central too often. The quest for affluence has become oppressive, and the problem cannot be cured by writing another check.

Consumerism without generosity. Years ago when careful planning was required to manage my family's very limited resources, we established a Barnabas fund. Named in honor of the generous "son of encouragement" in the Scriptures, the Barnabas fund was our giving account. The intent was to build up a balance in the account so we could not only meet our regular giving commitments but also be ready to respond spontaneously to people in need.

Generosity is an antidote to consumption. It transforms the drive to get more into the desire to give more. The practice of generosity turns the tables on the "I'm alive to acquire more stuff for me" syndrome. And the enriching experiences that flow out of giving to others can literally convert greed into gratitude.

Generosity also generates creativity. Surrendering our attention to others with the intent of responding to their need tunes us into our God-given frequencies to be givers and lovers. Then the best of life can flow from us creatively. Expressions of generosity come in many forms: handwritten letters, e-mails expressing encouragement, unexpected telephone calls, thoughtful compliments, a small appreciation gift, breakfast in bed, money for dinner at a quiet restaurant, time to be alone or to be with friends. When generosity flows, affluenza dissolves.

Independence without empathy. Living with financial stability in an economically developed society tends to nurture independence. But independence separates people from each other. Financial independence means people do not feel much need for each other. Spouses watch TV in separate rooms in the same house. Drivers travel alone, and penthouse residents take a private elevator up to a luxuriously furnished but people-empty apartment. As independent lifestyles become more entrenched, there is less empathy. The appeal of self-absorption increases.

Money is also a social divider. The haves are separated from the have-nots. Every democratic society will always have a range of economic levels and a variation of social structures. The point is not to try to create a utopia. But when our social privilege shuts down our empathy for those who are less fortunate, the affluenza fever rises.

Gratification now. One hundred years ago the pattern for purchasing goods was to work first and save money in order to lay down cash for the new acquisition. Paying on the installment plan was the next way to acquire major necessities. Instead of buying with saved-up cash, the strategy was to make payments with added interest for such items as automobiles and home mortgages. The plan was to "pay as you use" the goods and services.

The introduction of credit cards to the masses ushered in another pattern. In contrast to saving first or paying as purchases are used, credit card purchasing is an invitation to instant gratification. Instead of working to save money for obtaining what one desires, the credit card way is to enjoy the benefits immediately and work and pay later. An added incentive to buy first and pay later is the recent trend of the awarding of points. The possibility of accumulating points to get something for nothing is a marketing ploy to entice us to borrow more.

The point is obvious. When instant gratification rules, affluenza reigns.

Work without sabbaths. The commandment is clear: Don't work too much. Beware of your addictions. Remember the sabbath and be sure restoration is part of your rhythm. Back off and take a break. You and the people in your life will be better for it.

I wish it weren't true, but I am a sabbath breaker. I regularly make the case that God's ways are good and right and best, but I still transgress in this realm. I could offer a careful defense, but in the end my failure is not defensible. Maybe when I retire it will be different.

I'm not sure of all the reasons I never seem to have enough time.

Blaming the spirit of the age or the omnipresence of computers and modems does not adequately account for my incessant sin. I suspect it has more to do with some deeper insecurities related to earning enough to live with more than I really need.

DIRECTION FOR THE JOURNEY

John Wesley is credited with the stewardship maxim "Work as hard as you can; make as much as you can; spend as little as you can; give as much as you can." Wesley's approach will be a sound strategy for many of us who want to resist being co-opted by today's consumer culture.

We will also be helped to ward off the disease of affluenza and live with liberty as God energizes us to

- do well financially and be responsible
- live as faithful stewards of our gifts and of opportunities that will enable us to exist with dignity
- do good relationally and live generously
- live with imagination, looking for ways to respond to people with needs and surprise them with encouragement
- do good spiritually and give widely to the work of the kingdom
- live with a vision to support what God is doing to bring the hope of heaven to those who are broken
- do good socially and support causes selectively
- live with a commitment to be a cultural contributor

And when we see the power of money ruling the wills and ways of people around us, we can gently pray, "Grant that I may seek not so much to be understood as to understand."

8   Character Without Design

Some people's character is so deep they can live on automatic pilot. They consistently choose what is right and do what is good. Integrity marks their life. Other people's character is so shallow they use clouds on a windy day as omens for determining what is right and good. They weave here and there on their way through life's predicaments. Sometimes they are honorable; sometimes they are not.

The question is, Who am I when I'm alone with me? Who are you when you are the real you? When we surrender to the essence of our real self and true character, who lives there?

I believe that the vast majority of people would like integrity to mark their life. People get up in the morning wanting to do what is right and good. All around the world people prefer honesty over dishonesty and generosity over greed. Only a tiny percentage of humankind can stand in front of a mirror and readily say, "Today I want to be instrument of evil."

Still, translating our good intentions into commendable behavior can be difficult, especially in these times when we are often invited to let our personal preferences define what is right and good. Many of us could benefit from a few more rules and regulations, yet we are left to scramble our way through moral mazes. Here lies the point of vulnerability for people who aspire to goodness but are not prepared to adopt a defined set of values and a clear belief system. They want to be trustworthy people but are not prepared to surrender to established ways of living that are wiser than their own thoughts and ideas. They want character without design—coherent ethics for daily living without adequately resourcing their inner life.

An inner life that is not intentionally designed is like life in a house with no furniture and with no paintings hanging on the walls. The living space is incomplete. The building blocks of an informed conscience are absent. Some of the ingredients from which good character flows are missing. Although such people's efforts may produce a parade of achievements that stimulates their self-confidence, they will lose their way in the moral maze. Their miscalculation of what it takes to think straight and live right will result in their giving in to another enemy with a smiling face.

COLLAGE CULTURE

As missiologist Lesslie Newbigin notes, "It has become commonplace to say that we live in a pluralist society—not merely a society which is in fact plural in the variety of cultures, religions and lifestyles which it embraces, but pluralist in the sense that this plurality is celebrated as things to be approved and cherished."[1] Social changes inaugurated in the 1960s are reinforced by the assumptions of pluralism. But when there are many equally valid ways to believe and behave, social fragmentation is inevitable.

Gary Dorrien identifies one of the social shifts: "Many Americans no longer take moral instruction from character-shaping communities of any kind. The religious and republican moral languages of America's past are being displaced by an individualized pursuit of success or emotional satisfaction that places highly tenuous selves . . . at the center."[2]

Instead of presenting life as an integrated whole, the spirit of the age invites people to create a patchwork collage. A life can be assembled, as it were, with a pair of scissors and a glue stick: a scrap from my family history, a patch of my spiritual intuition, a piece of lofty historical philosophy, bits of counsel from my best friends, a short list of my personal goals, along with highlights from an Internet search for "What makes life worth living?"

A mystified young mother of my acquaintance looks at the randomness of life around her and laments, "I feel like I am heading out to play a role for which the script has been lost."

DEFAULTING TO SELF-INTEREST

Regrettably, the default moral compass setting in many people's lives is self-interest. Author Wendy Murray Zoba believes that our culture of consumerism fuels self-interest. She contends that the "consumerism mindset has convinced us that *our* narrative . . . is ours to write."[3]

Being motivated by self-interest may be increasing in these times, but it is not a new phenomenon. Two thousand years ago Jesus told a story that brought the issue of self-interest to the attention of his disciples:

> There was a rich man who had a manager, and charges were brought to him that this man was squandering his property. So he summoned him and said to him, "What is this that I hear about you? Give me an accounting of your management, because you cannot be my manager any longer." Then the manager said to himself, "What will I do, now that my master is taking the position away from me? I am not strong enough to dig, and I am ashamed to beg. I have decided what to do so that, when I am dismissed as manager, people may welcome me into their homes." So, summoning his master's debtors one by one, he asked the first, "How much do you owe my master?" He answered, "A hundred jugs of olive oil." He said to him, "Take your bill, sit down quickly, and make it fifty." Then he asked another, "And how much do you owe?" He replied, "A hundred containers of wheat." He said to him, "Take your bill and make it eighty." And his master commended the dishonest manager because he had acted shrewdly; for the children of this age are more shrewd in dealing with their own generation than are the children of light. (Lk 16:1-8)

On the one hand, self-interest can generate amazing creativity. Looking after me is exhilarating! Even the exploited master was impressed with the shrewdness of his dishonest manager. However, the downside was that the manager's self-interest tainted his ethics. Jesus doesn't spell out the sequel, but we can well imagine that the master sent out warnings to his debtors so they would not also be exploited.

One great flaw of self-interest is that we start believing we can live well on our own. The tendency to put self at the center distances us from persons and communities that are important to our well-being. Author Thomas Friedman wisely points out, "You cannot be a complete person alone. You can be a rich person alone. You can be a smart person alone. But you cannot be a complete person alone."[4] We will not find personal meaning by continually disregarding others and defaulting to self-interest.

Those who insist on defaulting to self-interest will live handicapped lives. They will spend so much time and effort looking after themselves that they will cut themselves off from people who would like to spend time enjoying and enriching them.

FURNISHED MINDS, CONSTRUCTED CONSCIENCES

Sociologist Robert Wuthnow points us in the right direction: "For the soul to be compelling, it must be rooted in authoritative traditions that transcend the person and point to larger realities in which the person is embedded."[5]

To live well, everyone needs a furnished home: a mind that has reference points, touchstones, boundaries, and trustworthy sources and people to assist with life's decisions. In our collage culture, just as virtues need definition so also vices need definition. We all need criteria for making judgment calls. Otherwise we are left with random impulses and subjective opinions. Our world is too complex for us to be left alone with decisions that can have detrimental effects on ourselves and others we care about.

Good practices come from good theory. And good theory is rooted in sources beyond the imagination and calculation of any one person or any single generation. To ignore historical sources of wisdom, trustworthy advisers, and systems of thought and guidance that have proven their worth over time amounts to uninformed arrogance.

We also need a carefully constructed conscience, built of informed convictions and the capacity to make moral choices. We require consciences with functioning traffic lights—green, yellow and red—to give direction at the moral intersections of our days and nights.

"Conscience is the ethical compass of character," says theologian Larry Rasmussen.[6] Admittedly, it is difficult to always follow the direction the compass charts for us. Sometimes ethical complexity and ambiguous circumstances cause the needle to waver back and forth so that we can't get a foolproof reading. But in the long run, people who have deliberately rooted themselves in principles and convictions are the people who more consistently match their behavior with their good intentions.

For all of us, life's challenge goes beyond providing for our needs and piling up achievements. The bigger issue is how we live and work along the way. There is no real success without self-respect. And self-respect will elude us unless we can discern the color of the traffic light at our life's moral intersections.

The ebb and flow of life brings us all kinds of opportunities to demonstrate the presence or absence of furnished minds and constructed consciences. Whether we are showered with accolades, alienated from members of our family, jilted by a lover, treated unfairly, offered a promotion at work that really belongs to a colleague, fired unjustly from a long-term job or betrayed by a treasured friend, we are faced with decisions and dilemmas about what to think and how to act. At the intersections we assess the alternatives, make decisions and take action.

BEING OUR BEST SELVES

The preferred response is to be our best selves. Sports columnist Rick Reilly contends,

> There's never been a finer man in American sports than John Wooden, or a finer coach. He won 10 NCAA basketball championships at UCLA. . . . Nobody has ever come within six of him. He

won 88 straight games. . . . Nobody has come within 42 since.
. . . Of the 180 players who played for him, Wooden knows the
whereabouts of 172. . . . "Discipline yourself, and others won't
need to," Coach would say. "Never lie, never cheat, never steal,"
Coach would say. "Earn the right to be proud and confident."

Wooden was almost ninety at the time of Reilly's profile, and it had been
"15 years since Nellie, his beloved wife of 53 years, died. In her memory,
he sleeps only on his half of the bed, only on his pillow, only on top of
the sheets, never between, with just the old bedspread they shared to
keep him warm. 'I'm not afraid to die,' he says. 'Death is my only chance
to be with her again.'"[7]

What a tribute—even if it is only telling one side of the story. On the
virtue side on the ledger of Coach Wooden's life are discipline and a high
regard for relationships. His ethical boundaries are fused into his inner
self, and his framework for leading others is clear. His life is compelling
because he is rooted in strong beliefs and defined convictions that are beyond his own making. His character has design.

GETTING ORIENTED TO AMBIGUITY

Obviously, some measure of self-interest is both healthy and necessary.
God's Great Commandment invites us to find a balance between loving
our neighbors and loving ourselves. The challenge is to walk the balance.
Too much of self at the center of life produces excessive selfishness
and leaves too little room for others. At the other extreme, too little regard for self leads to excessive dependence on others, their views, their
expectations and their approval. Walking the self-others balance takes
energy, creates complexity and generates ambiguity.

In our age thoughtful people cannot escape an array of ambiguity-gen-
erating, technologically fed ethical dilemmas. The mere mention of genetic
engineering, gene technology, birth technology and fetal research makes
most of us feel there is too much to comprehend. Past generations lived in
a milieu where there was little debate about the definition of a family and
where the moral lines for sexual behavior were clearly drawn. Today de-

bates about family forms continue unresolved, and the right to choose any of various ways of expressing one's sexuality is firmly established.

People who live without touchstones and boundaries, without a furnished mind or a conscience with design, are destined for increasing ambiguity. Howard Marshall observes that "to some people maturity seems to mean questioning everything and being agnostic on all things. Surely, however, the mark of maturity is to arrive at firm convictions instead of remaining forever in an attitude of adolescent questioning and scepticism."[8]

The challenge, again, is to walk in balance. On the one hand, we can live with a self-understanding of "I am unfinished and have more to learn." On the other hand, we should hold some ideas and beliefs so firmly that we are comfortable with a closed mind—hold some convictions that are certain enough to say, "I've spent enough time deciding what I believe on that subject, and now I'm figuring out how to live accordingly."

Those who keep struggling to walk in balance will not escape ambiguity, but they will keep moving toward maturity.

RESISTING DARKNESS

Living without a framework or a faith takes its toll. When we are less and less certain about what is right and good, we are increasingly left to drift in the direction of our natural inclinations. Which is the strongest pull? Do we defer to behavioral patterns of self-interest, do we draw upon the capacities of our best self, or do we run the risk of surrendering to the darkness of our worst self?

One does not have to believe the Bible to conclude that the darkness of evil is real. Osama Bin Laden's videotaped harangues, entrenched hatred in Jerusalem and Palestine, ethnic cleansing, vile exchanges between spouses seeking sole custody of their children, the sexual abuse of women, random violence in schools and the senseless killing of innocent people are all definitive proof.

Professor James Garbarino of Cornell University, author of *Lost Boys*, exposes evil in the lives of the young boys he has studied: "These boys fall victim to an unfortunate synchronicity between the demons inhabiting their own internal world and the corrupting influences of modern American culture: vicarious violence, crude sexuality, shallow materialism, mean-spirited competitiveness and spiritual emptiness."[9] We cannot deny what is real; human beings have the capacity to perpetrate horrendous acts of evil on each other.

There is a vast apparent difference between blatant evil and what we might call "restrained evil." Blatant evil is described by Jeremiah. People "acted shamefully . . . yet they were not ashamed, they did not know how to blush" (Jer 6:15). People who deal out blatant evil have lost their human capacity to have moral feelings. They maim and destroy, but their tragedy is that somewhere along their journey their morality died.

Restrained evil is more sophisticated. It is carefully calculated, less public but more frequent. It involves getting even, embarrassing people, taking credit that belongs to someone else and putting others down in order to take a step up. Purveyors of restrained evil kill other people's reputations while they escape without a criminal record. The paths of pain they inflict on others may escape public scrutiny, but in their inner being the perpetrators know they are wrong.

Cornelius Plantinga Jr. states, "All sin is equally wrong, but not all sin is equally bad."[10] The real point is that all sin is wrong *and* bad. It is destructive and life-denying. And people who live without the protection of a furnished mind and the restraints of a constructed conscience are more susceptible to both blatant evil and restrained evil than those who surrender to beliefs that transcend their own perceptions.

If you choose the Christian way, the opposite extreme of surrendering to darkness is centering on the God of creation and the Christ of redemption. It is also to surrender to the counsel of the Scriptures:

> For the grace of God has appeared, bringing salvation to all, training us to renounce impiety and worldly passions, and in the present age to live lives that are self-controlled, upright, and godly, while we wait for the blessed hope and the manifestation of the glory of our great God and Savior, Jesus Christ. (Tit 2:11-13)

Renouncing worldly passions, impiety and evil in the present age may sound like a highly improbable course to take. Living a life that is self-controlled, upright and godly may not even be on your map of possibilities. But a life that is centered on God is meant to attract us into unexplored territory. Lawrence Cunningham offers good counsel: "When our faith is tested to the point where God may seem absent, it is at that dark moment when God may be drawing us closer to him."[11]

These are not easy days in which to keep our faith focus unentangled from negative social trends. But each previous time had its particular difficulties as well. Martin Luther is an example of one of God's people challenged by the status quo of faith and the great issues of his times. His faith commitments were energized by his alert mind and rooted convictions. His words are particularly apt for our times: "My conscience is captive to the Word of God; to go against conscience is neither right nor safe; here I stand, there is nothing else I can do; God help me; amen."[12]

Contemporary followers of God are called to venture into the current age with the knowledge that it is captive to the same Word of God that spoke in past times. We are called to furnish our mind with thoughtful beliefs and our conscience with careful convictions in order to live faithfully in the ambiguity of these times. And we are called to stand, without a sense of superiority, with the saints.

DIRECTION FOR THE JOURNEY

A recent television advertisement for a bank included the slogan "Imagine what the world would be like—if people made promises and kept them." The trouble is that too many people do not have the capacity to keep their promises. They have been undermined by a serious miscalculation. Without surrendering to God's design, they thought that on their own they could reach the lofty heights reserved for those of noble character. Instead they are left to live in the shadows with their incomplete self. Their ambivalent character keeps them in the grasp of an enemy with a smiling face. They are victims of their miscalculation that their own resources alone are adequate to allow them to live well.

Just as pictures need frames to set off their beauty, we need frames to live to our full God-ordained potential. We need a mind that has reference points, touchstones, boundaries and trustworthy sources to assist with life's decisions. We need a carefully constructed conscience with the capacity to make informed moral choices. We need to be rooted in a deeper reality than just ourselves so that our character can be designed with wisdom—wisdom that produces behavior that deserves to be respected.

Along the way, as we encounter people without touchstones and boundaries and others who claim to have life all figured out but whose behavior does not deserve to be respected, may our response be gracious: "Grant that I may seek not so much to be understood as to understand."

9 Privatized Faith

While shopping for Christmas presents in a small store I had no choice but to overhear a most interesting conversation. A woman entered the store and met an acquaintance she had not seen for some time. They exchanged enthusiastic greetings and began sharing their plans for celebrating Christmas. After comparing notes on the parties, concerts and the size of turkey to be purchased, one of the women said, "And we always make a point of going to church at Christmas time."

She then excitedly announced that her son was getting married. Her friend discreetly asked how she viewed her son's fiancée. The mother replied, "I've only met her once. She looks like a good match for our son. We are pleased. She is a delightful young woman, and she has a great string of convictions."

That was the first and only time I've heard the expression "She has a great string of convictions." Later I wondered why the woman used those particular words. Why didn't the mother say, "Her religious convictions are important to her" or "The principles of her faith are central in her life"?

Perhaps the reason is rooted in the presence of *privatized faith*. Perhaps the mother's family attends church only occasionally—Christmas and Easter. She gives the Christian faith some ongoing place in her life. She knows it is important for spouses in a marriage to have convictions. However, being a follower of Jesus is not her primary concern; she does not generally see life in a Christian framework. Her identity includes being a Christian, and her concerns are right and real, but her language has been stripped of anything overtly religious.

What may be surprising is that this mother represents approximately half of the adults who live in North America.[1] Those who make up this social segment may not be aware of their spiritual standing in today's society, but they can be named and described as "privatized faith Christians."

TRAITS OF PRIVATIZED FAITH

Novelist Stephen King in his autobiographical book *On Writing* comes close to describing the attitude of privatized faith Christians: "While I believe in God, I have no use for organized religion."[2] Softening one word in King's statement makes it an accurate description of the way most privatized faith people feel: "While I believe in God, I have *little* use for organized religion."

People who claim to believe in God but give organized religion little or no role in their life are living with an enemy with a smiling face. They turn faith that is meant to be experienced in community into a private affair.

CENSUS CHRISTIANS

When census data collectors or telephone poll researchers ask individuals to identify their religion, privatized faith people immediately answer, "Christian." Whether they attend church or not, when asked "What denomination or church do you belong to?" privatized faith Christians proceed to name a denomination or Christian tradition.[3]

Some of God's faithful people contend that privatized faith or census Christians do not merit being called Christian at all. In their mind, what is absent is more important than what is present: "There is no claim or evidence of their personal relationship with Jesus Christ." Other Christians reason, "Who are we to judge? One's faith is a private affair. The church is filled with hypocrites anyway. Faith is a matter to be decided between individuals and their God."

Whatever our perspective may be on census Christians, we can paint their profile. The absence of regular church participation does distance them from well-established patterns of spiritual commitment. Because North America has a dominant Christian history, in all likelihood today's privatized faith Christians have simply assumed the religious identification of their parents. Their faith has probably been cradled in their family and cultural upbringing. Whether or not their faith is the result of a reflective personal process can be known only on an individual basis. But by definition, census Christians are passive theists, not active atheists. They may be religiously apathetic, but they are not opposed to basic Christian views and values. They may be nominal Christians, but they are not part of an anti-Christian cultural conspiracy.

Using Ireland as a darkly humorous example, Peter Berger illustrates the dark side of countries with a Christian history that are populated with census Christians. As a man walks down a dark street in Belfast, a gunman jumps out of a doorway, holds a gun to his head and asks, "Are you Protestant or Catholic?"

The man stutters, "Well, actually, I'm an atheist."

"Ah yes," says the gunman, "but are you a Protestant or a Catholic atheist?"[4]

In North America, the Christian statistical indicators remain relatively stable, but the social influence of the faith is in decline. Still, as we attempt to discern the implications, it is more accurate to lament the loss of God than to mourn the death of God.

CEREMONIAL CHRISTIANS

Our home is situated on a small street with ten other houses. There are no traffic jams on Sunday morning as we back out of our driveway to head off to church. Consistent with Canada's church attendance demographic, there is just one other family on the street that is involved regularly with a faith community. On a comparable street in the United States, four houses would hold families that were frequent church attenders.

Parking is readily available on a normal Sunday at our church. However, several times a year when we arrive at our regular time, the church parking lot is already full. If I've had a deep sleep the night before and time for a leisurely second cup of coffee, my response is close to what it ought to be: "Today is baptism Sunday. We get to welcome new members into our faith family." Sometimes, though, my reaction is to groan inwardly: *The "hatch, match and dispatch" crowd—the ceremonial Christians—are here. I wonder how many babies and how much longer the service will last.* My parking-lot reaction determines whether my preworship prayer is full of praise or of confession.

Ceremonial Christians are people who activate their census Christian claims every now and then. They are almost unchurched and give the impression of being occasional Christians. In the back of their mind, ceremonial Christians believe the church exists to provide the sacred rites of passage related to baptism, marriage and death. Accordingly, they can rationalize the integrity of their Christian identity without the need for regular church participation. Regrettably, they are users of religious privileges rather than contributors to the vitality of organized religious life.

Ceremonial Christians are card-carrying Christians. They are like those who carry in their wallet a current Visa card that they rarely use. The unfortunate result is that neither the company issuing the card nor the person carrying it receives the benefits for which the system was designed.

Still, whenever ceremonial Christians use their card, that is evidence of the presence of the Spirit and a quiet desire for the things of God in them. Clergy and church leaders are right to continue to experiment with ways to offer the sacred rites as a way to try to connect with these people.

CUSTOMIZED CHRISTIANS

Accurately reading the continuing role of religion in North American life, Wendy Doniger concludes, "The human race will stay married to religion, in sickness and in health, for richer or poorer, for better or for worse. But now it will be an open marriage."[5] I interpret "open marriage" here to mean a marriage without the need for a lifetime covenant to one partner, a marriage that is subject to renegotiation on more favorable terms. After all, the spirit of the age invites us to indulge in the creation of our own spiritualities and to customize our faith.

Customized believers are independent believers. They assemble their beliefs as if they were putting together the component parts of a music system. Customized believers may or may not have high praise for Jesus. They may or may not belong to a church or faith community; for them it's a matter of personal taste. Their spirits resonate with the claim that "faith teaches that there is an eternal heartbeat in me that belongs to God."[6] Accordingly, they let their experience validate their heartbeats of faith and believe what works for them. They live off fragments of faith—a piece here and a taste there.

COMMITTED CHRISTIANS

Census, ceremonial and customized Christians all have virtues that must not be discounted. But neither should their deficiencies remain unnamed. They are wilderness Christians. Instead of being planted by rivers of life-giving water, their roots are placed in ground that in the long run will become more and more arid.

Proposing that census, ceremonial and customized Christians are all people with privatized faith leaves us with the need to define "committed Christians." Religious sociologists Rodney Stark and Charles Glock serve as insightful theologians by linking "being religious" to five dimensions: embracing belief, practice, knowledge, experience and consequences. Their framework begins to define what it means to be a committed Christian.

Stark and Glock define their five dimensions as follows. *Embracing belief* means that the religious person will hold a certain theological outlook and acknowledge the truth of the tenets of the religion. *Practice* includes church attendance, taking Communion and participating in a church community. Religious people's *knowledge* means they possess some minimum of information about the basic tenets of faith and its rites, scriptures and traditions. *Experience* means that "religious persons will at some time and in some way make a direct subjective contact with the divine . . . that the person will experience communication of some kind with God in a transcendental way." And all of this has *consequence:* effects of beliefs, practice, experience and knowledge are seen in a person's daily life.[7]

Both explicitly and implicitly, theologian Karl Rahner injects energy into the five dimensions by declaring:

> Christianity is love of one's neighbor, and a love of one's neighbor which draws its ultimate strength from liberating contemplation of the crucified and risen Christ. Through these experiences we come to know what is meant when we say "God." . . . The essential Christianity can't stay at the level of theory in people's heads or of Sunday sermons, but has to become life-immediate, realistic, and habitual—at the heart of the "secular" daily round.[8]

Stark and Glock's model would not be adequate for serious theologians, but it does help us distinguish between the incompleteness of the various expressions of privatized faith and the holistic substance of commitment faith.

A GREAT RELIGIOUS SHIFT

What happened in North America that shifted the cultural balance of religious life from a majority of committed Christians to a majority of privatized faith Christians? Why did many Christian citizens become so disillusioned with their involvement in organized church life that they chose to disengage from the institutions they once valued? A complete answer is not possible here, but there are some major reasons to note.

First of all, the shift from committed to privatized happened over time. The shift is partly about the story of families. Three generations ago, the vast majority of North American families went to church on a regular basis together. Two generations ago, increasing numbers of parents sent their children to Sunday school and church rather than attending with them. The pattern today is that parents who were sent to church on their own do not send their children, nor do they attend themselves. But at census and ceremonial times, the roots of their faith are still strong enough for them to identify as Christians and desire the sacred rites of passage. Again, the Canadian shift is more pronounced, but the patterns also apply generally to the United States.

During the decades when the balance of religious life was shifting, increasing secularization of the public forum drove religion into the private realm. Restrictions on using public buildings for religious purposes and debates about praying in public places or using the name of Jesus Christ at civic or sporting events are not just examples of socially separating the church and state, they are also indicators of increasing secularization. Catholic scholar Hervé Carrier observes that populations that were Christianized in the past now live in secularized climates where they are socially marginalized—where religion is devalued and believers and their communities are marginalized.[9] In times like these, committed Christians stay their spiritual courses, while privatized faith people tend to go with the social trends set by the majority.

Another cultural impetus that moved people into the space of privatized faith was the demotion of the institutional and the promotion of the individual. Stated another way, the appeal of interpersonal relationships and individual interests preempted the desire to be involved in organizational structures. The flow of culture shifted away from ascribing importance to formally belonging, and informal ways of relating have been increasingly embraced. Rather than having made commitments to organizational agendas and signed membership cards, belonging now means to be somewhere with people who know you by name and welcome you into their circle.

VCRs and later DVDs symbolize the social shift. In the past, individuals and families could watch a movie only in the formal setting of a theater. They had to organize their lives around the theater's schedule. Today people are more apt to self-schedule. They do what they want, with whom they want, when they want. If a program they want to watch on television airs at an inconvenient time, they simply record the program so it can be viewed later. This gravitational pull toward designing life around one's personal preferences nurtured the dispositions of privatized faith people, who were already ambivalent about their involvement in a place of worship.

Cultural analyst and sociologist Robert Wuthnow speaks in defense of our religious institutions: "People do not expect to govern themselves without political institutions; they cannot earn their livelihoods without economic institutions; they even cannot participate in their 'private' leisure activities, such as reading books, playing golf, or watching television without the benefit of social institutions. Religious life should be no different."[10]

RESISTING CULTURAL PLURALISM

These have been difficult decades for many churches and their leaders. In the past, the wider culture itself was a delivery system to bring parishioners into their sanctuaries. In some areas the Christian voice was not just the dominant voice but an unchallenged voice. Today the entrenchment of cultural pluralism means the Christian alternative is just one option within a chorus of competing options.

The emergence of cultural pluralism often appeared as a threat to churches and committed Christians. Instead of accepting social and moral diversity as a given of God's creation and a necessity of democracy, too many churches deemed cultural pluralism an enemy of the faith and entered into culture wars. The better strategy would have been to affirm the need for social structures to cradle our cultural diversity, making room for concerned Christians to be faithful to their convictions as well as creating space for those whom God allows to live in other ways.

A historic opportunity to be truly Christian was missed by church leaders who either attempted to deny cultural space to people who held different views from their own or missed carving out distinctive cultural space for Christians to take their spiritual stand. They engaged neither the people in the world nor the privatized faith Christians who were watching from the sidelines.

On the one hand, the conservative church leaders who interpreted cultural pluralism as an enemy were so judgmental and mean-spirited that they distanced themselves from the more accepting privatized faith people. They didn't understand that a genuinely pluralistic culture puts all beliefs on the same level, which opens up opportunities for witness and evangelism to highlight Christianity's uniqueness within the chorus of options.[11]

On the other hand, the accommodating Christian leaders who failed to offer Christ's uniqueness and sufficient clarity of truth and conscience left the privatized faith people pretty much where they already were—watching from the sidelines. Alice Camille articulates the needed challenge: "Not to embrace Christ the King is to continue to bow before the countless sovereigns of the world and to light sacrifices at too many altars. Not to listen to Christ is to face the schizophrenia of voices beckoning, demanding, cajoling our obedience, all the while spinning their web of half-truths."[12]

DIRECTION FOR THE JOURNEY

I went to church today. It's an old church, a good church, but far from a perfect church. Worship at my church centers me. It reminds me who God is and why Jesus is still the way, the truth and the life. Sometimes worship warms my spirit, and sometimes it probes and prods me. Sometimes I'm just glad when the benediction is next in the order of service.

Confession is the gift that invites me to begin again. Prayer puts me in my place. When I leave the sanctuary I know that God is the Creator and I am just one of the created, still in the process of working out my salvation. The sermon anchors me in the past and offers direction not only for how to live in the moment but also for what is coming around the next corner. The sacrament feeds my soul. Jesus meets me there.

My church involvement means I cannot forget how big the world really is and how much spiritual and human need is out there. The compassionate services to forgotten people, the sick, the abused, the dysfunctional and those who just can't make it on their own humble me and make me grateful. I love being a part of something divine—something that is a lot bigger than me.

People know me by name at church. They ask me, "How is it going?" and then wait for an answer. They celebrate my joys and prop me up when I need their care. I can call them on the phone without feeling as if I'm interrupting.

If you were to take church out of the pattern of my life, I would worry about my spiritual future. I'm afraid I would get centered on things that don't deserve to be trusted and worshiped. I wonder how long it would be before I felt myself shifting from being a committed Christian into the patterns of being a privatized faith Christian.

I remember another church service I attended. It was a mass in a language I couldn't understand in Dar es Salaam, Tanzania. The large church was full, and people were actively participating. Almost everything about the worship was unfamiliar to me. I was more of an observer than a participant. About halfway through the pastor's sermon, a woman walked up the aisle with a young child, looking for a place to sit. I wondered to myself, *What could her story be? Why is she so late? Why did she come?* Then the insight of the hour arrived: It is better to arrive late to church than not to arrive at all. This is true for census, ceremonial and customized Christians—the privatized faith people. It is better to arrive late than not to arrive at all.

Prayer: Finding the Heart's True Home, Richard Foster's popular book on prayer, opens with a passionate statement about our human and insatiable longing for home. "For too long, we have been in a far country: a country of noise and hurry and crowds, a country of climb and push and shove, a country of frustration and fear and intimidation. God welcomes us home, home to serenity and peace and joy, home to friendship and fellowship and openness, home to intimacy and acceptance and affirmation."[13]

For those who resist coming home—home to personal trust in Christ, an imperfect but caring community of faith, a church where people know you by name and take time to listen to how you really are—I pray, "Grant that I may seek not so much to be understood as to understand."

PART 3

LEARNING TO RELATE TO ENEMIES
WITH SMILING FACES

*Grant that I may seek not so much
to be right as to relate.*

All of us who live on God's good earth are subject to vulnerabilities. For example, many of us are prone to believing that because "we are right," those who view life through other lenses are of necessity "wrong." Or because we are white or Asian or African American, we feel that our cultural ways are superior to those of other ethnic groups. Why else does the practice of naming ourselves as Christians lead so naturally to labeling others as "non-Christians"? We may not like admitting it, but we have the capacity to downsize life, to reduce others down to our self-size. The practice is sometimes termed *ethnocentrism*. The behavior leads to cultural containment.

Self-sizing leads to the desire to reduce the social space of others down to our personal preferences. We attempt to restrict the rights and privileges of individuals around us to our particular views and values or to our specific version of the faith. When we live successfully as self-sizers, we tend to feel superior. We get comfortable with our self-righteousness and find it easy to invalidate the claims of others. Rather than making an effort to be inclusive, we justify being exclusive. We become "one product people," and if we were able to do away with the competition, we would still sleep soundly at night.

Restricting the rights of others, however we justify it, inevitably leads to social tensions: discrimination, racism, religious arrogance and blatant superiority. Politically, self-sizing generates the desire to dominate: "You are either with us or against us." Socially, self-sizing seeks to control: "Either become like us or find some other place to exist." Religiously, self-sizing demands conformity: "Believe and behave as we believe and behave or suffer the wrath of God."

The Scriptures summon us to be bigger than ourselves. Cornelius, a God-loving Gentile, was the man God used to break Peter out of his ethnic, spiritual and cultural containment. Cornelius was "a centurion of the Italian Cohort, as it was called. He was a devout man who feared God with all his household; he gave alms generously to the people and prayed constantly to God" (Acts 10:1-2).

Peter had a vision in which God told him to "kill and eat" animals that for Peter as a faithful Jew were unclean. "While Peter was greatly puzzled about what to make of the vision that he had seen, suddenly the men sent by Cornelius appeared. . . . Then Peter began to speak to them: 'I truly understand that God shows no partiality, but in every nation anyone who fears him and does what is right is acceptable to him'" (Acts 10:13-14, 17, 34-35).

Before encountering Cornelius, Peter was living with downsized, self-sized perceptions. It was as if he lived in a house with several windows letting light in from more than one direction, but his view was limited to what he could see out of just one window. Fortunately, God had a larger vision for Peter. God disrupted Peter's sleep and said, "Come with me. I want you to see something you've never seen before. I want you to look out of another window. I want to show you a fuller picture of what life is supposed to be."

The chapters in the following section pull back the curtains and look out of a number of windows. We will wrestle with our shared tendency to self-size life—that is, to reduce life down to my size. What does Jesus' "golden rule," to treat others as we would like to be treated, really mean?

10 Dealing with Diversity

The country where we are born nurtures us, influences us and contributes to shaping us. Being born in Canada has certainly left its imprint on me. Living in an economically prosperous country has meant I experience many of my wants as "needs." Being part of a nation of only thirty million people takes away any temptation to dream about being a major player on the global stage. Canada's disposition to mediate and deploy soldiers as peacemakers encourages me toward pacifism. Our English and French bilingualism has made me appreciate how important language is in preserving the distinctives of any culture. Our formal policy of multiculturalism sensitizes me to the need to respect ethnic and religious diversity. The nation's commitment to universal healthcare means that I'm ready to pay high taxes as a reasonable price for that social safety net privilege without complaining—at least most of the time.

People who have been born and live in the United States also get influenced. I suspect that to be fully American is to not only accept the "American way" as the best way but also to assume that people who live in other nations would benefit by embracing the American way. Surely there is a correlation between a nation's being born in revolution and struggling through a civil war and the propensity toward liberal gun laws. Perhaps because early colonizers came to America in pursuit of religious freedom, there exists the continued cultural belief in a "divine destiny," the assumption that God is on America's side. We should not be surprised that when American men and women go off to war the nation bows down in prayer. Further, the nation's collective confidence translates into individual dispositions to take risks and lead with confidence. In fact, Americans' cultural self-image and unchallenged global power are part of the reason American Christians are confident in sharing their faith. They assume it only makes sense to convert to the American versions of faith and life.

If you and I had been born in one of the postcommunist countries, our self-perceptions would be quite different. Our self-concept would be suffering from our having been reduced to means of production. Instead of celebrating the image of God and our spiritual giftedness, we would be struggling to find enough self-regard to motivate personal initiative. We would have to deal with the personal and social consequences of a massive breakdown in moral and spiritual values. Our respect for property rights and the common good would lack coherent reference points. And we might well wonder, *If Communism was so bad, why are our social and economic circumstances worse now than they were before?* If we had survived a war, we would likely be more drawn to despair than to hope.

When you walk into the historic walled city of Dubrovnik, Croatia, you are confronted with a large map showing every building inside the walls. The site of each Serbian shell that hit a building in the 1991 war is clearly recorded. So that the Croats do not forget the pain inflicted on them by warring terrorists, symbols indicate the places where shrapnel dispersed, fires spread destruction, and shells left craters in the road. The inscription under the map is sobering: "We will never forgive them for attacking our sacred city!" The people of Dubrovnik are thus encouraged to play mental reruns of violence and retell their stories of pain.

My spirit was moved in a much different way when I watched a television documentary recounting the story of the "Little Rock Nine." The dramatic portrayal of the nine black teenage high school students whose valor resulted in the 1957 racial integration in Mississippi's Central High

School made me believe that other injustices can also be resolved. In my view, their courage and readiness to withstand insult and racial hatred qualify them for sainthood. When the documentary showed President Dwight Eisenhower intervening to implement the Supreme Court ruling asserting the authority of federal over state law, I literally stood up and exclaimed, "Thanks be to God." The words of poet Maya Angelou, who was a young leader in the movement for racial justice at the time, deserve to be inscribed above the doors of the state legislature: "We should all know that diversity makes for a rich tapestry, that all the threads of the tapestry are equal in value."

Sadly, religion has often encouraged exclusion and violence rather than the courage of the Little Rock Nine. As Angela Ellis-Jones notes, "Intensely religious societies tend to be unpleasant places for those who do not share the faith."[1] It is true that historical roots of religion are often mixed with political and other cultural influences. Still, faith is at least part of the fuel that feeds the entrenched hatred between Protestants and Catholics in Ireland, the readiness of Muslims and Christians to abuse each other in Indonesia, and the targeted violence between Hindus and Muslims in India. Although the degree of physical violence may be less in North America, the name of God is readily invoked to rain down moral judgment and categorically denounce the validity of religious groups that are different from our own, even within the Christian faith. Protestant preachers feel free to denounce the doctrines and ritual practices of Catholics and fellow Protestants who deviate from their own cherished "biblical" interpretations. Catholic cardinals resist acknowledging the legitimacy of the Protestant Reformation and continue to declare their church to be the one true church. Why do many people of faith feel compelled to judge other religious organizations only according to their own doctrines and practices?

I participated recently in an ecumenical consultation that involved Anglican, Catholic, Orthodox, Pentecostal, historic Protestant and evangelical Christians. We were looking for common ground and ways to work together. During the discussion, the issue of how we understand the church became our focus. We heard a high-level Vatican Catholic voice reaffirm the Roman Catholic Church's long-established apostolic standing in God's kingdom. When pressed to make more room for other Christian traditions and denominations, the appeal was, "Please extend to us the right to define ourselves as we have believed through the centuries."

During the coffee break, I had a hallway discussion with a Russian Orthodox Church representative. We reflected on the previous conversations, and then I said, "I can only assume that if the Catholics take their prerogative to self-define and the Orthodox do the same, then it is the prerogative of Protestants to affirm their distinctive views too."

I was caught off guard when he responded, "Well, no. The Orthodox Church is the true church."

The ensuing conversation that distinguished between agreeing with each other and accepting each other brought a little light into the corridor—but only a little. There is heavy traffic on the "I am right, you have to be wrong" religious highway.

I remember an experience drinking tea at a small table in India. We were discussing the role of churches in that community. I asked, "How many churches are here?" and was told, "There are none." My host explained that people from a Pentecostal church sometimes visited the community to do street preaching, but they did not have a church building in the immediate area.

A few minutes later as we were walking in the community, we passed a rather large Catholic church. I was surprised and commented, "Did I understand you to say there were no churches in this community?"

My gracious and articulate host understood my probe and quietly responded, "Oh, the Catholics; they pray to Mary, you know."

Whether the issues involve political power, social equality or religious perceptions, the human family is being tormented by power-hungry political self-interest, blatant ethnic arrogance and religious small-mindedness. How can we deal with our diversity without inflicting pain on each other? Is it possible to create frameworks that invite us to be true to ourselves without denigrating others who are different? How can we learn to relate in positive ways to those who downsize life to their ethnocentric self-sizes?

SOCIETY STRATEGIES

Let's readily acknowledge that even though we desire equality, equal affirmation for all forms of diversity is not possible. There is too much evil roaming the world for us to surrender our discernment to blanket permissiveness. Beyond the limits defined by our criminal codes, we must reserve the right to declare some actions morally wrong and socially unacceptable. And as we seek to deal peaceably and productively with the disarray of diversity swirling around us, we must continue to address the tension between individual rights and social responsibility.

The beliefs that people embrace, the customs and rituals they practice, the views and values they translate into behaviors, the attitudes they nurture and the lifestyles they express make up a composite that shapes their national culture. We are like children on a massive playground where there are too few swings, slides, monkey bars and toilets to accommodate everyone. How can we make room for members of every culture to play on the playground?

Ethnic cleansing. The ethnic cleansing approach to life on the playground posts large KEEP OUT and DO NOT ENTER signs at the entrance gate. When any undesirables make their way inside and are discovered, they are socially marginalized, deported to another playground or lined up in front of a firing squad. Intolerance of outside influences is assumed to be the norm.

Sometimes attitudes of ethnic cleansing are seen in self-appointed playground patrols who feel called to be agents of moral cleansing. Their vision for life is to keep everyone's behavior within the boundaries they impose.

Melting pot. The melting-pot approach to life on the playground keeps the rules and regulations in the hands of the people in power. Most often they are the ruling majority who legally registered the playground for their use in the first place. The melting-pot mindset allows for differences, but only within limits. The drive is to melt down life on the playground to the preferences of the dominant group.

Aboriginal leader Ovide Mercredi takes issue with those who believe that "equality means everyone must be the same and that differences in lifestyle, culture, language and religion should be ignored if we are to share a democratic society." Unless democracy includes respect for differences and permission for diversity, the end result is assimilation—everyone becomes part of the dominant culture, and other cultural distinctives are lost.[2]

Cultural mosaic. The cultural mosaic approach to living in the playground allows people to bring their games and toys into the playing area and find a place to set them up. The disposition is to nurture a hybrid culture with a common core. In the cultural mosaic, diversity is celebrated, multicultural policies protect minorities, and people are encouraged to retain their ethnic distinctions. The assumption is that eventually people will share their ways with each other and everyone will be enriched.

The democratic challenge of the cultural mosaic over time is to determine what changes can be made to the common core. For example, how many different kinds of family structures should be allowed to coexist on the playground?

DISCERNING OUR PRINCIPLES

If we hold the conviction that everyone should be able to find their place in the playground, we are faced with the personal and social need to create space for others. Our challenge is to be true to ourselves while holding positive views toward those around us who have come to different conclusions about life. There are some principles to affirm and practices to follow.

God as the author of diversity. In the beginning, God did not paint a one-color world. The rainbow evidences God's love for creativity and the beauty of diversity. The separation of night from day, the sun, moon and stars, the shades of green that fill forests and plains, the countless animal species that grace the globe and the pantheon of the world's peoples all reveal God's love for diversity. The drama between good and evil in the Garden of Eden arose out of God's saying, in effect, "I don't believe in a one-way world. Human dignity is possible only when there are alternatives from which to choose."

We should not be surprised that God has also designed diversity into church life. When we think of the church, says Stan Gaede, "we must conjure up a picture not of people like ourselves, but of people of all colors and shapes and ages, women and men speaking different tongues, following different customs, practicing different habits, but all worshiping the same Lord."[3] Pastor Rick Warren sees this diversity as a strength: "No single church can possibly reach everyone. It takes all kinds of churches to reach all kinds of people."[4]

Instead of lamenting our differences and agonizing about the multi-mindedness from which there is no escape, we can take a deep breath and recognize God as the author of diversity.

Defend the right of cultural space for others. If God has etched diversity into creation, then those who deny the expression of diversity have got it wrong. So instead of denying cultural space to those whose views and values counter our own, we should ensure that they have the right to hold and express their preferences.

This line of logic seems to oppose the basic human instinct of self-protection. But that is the surprise factor God is inviting us to explore. Instead of simply making sure our interests are protected in God's design for life, we are also to reflect on the rights of others.

Stated in another way, people of faith must be students and practitioners of justice. Don Eberly points out that the pursuit of justice provides many opportunities for exemplary individual action.

When public action is committed to a pursuit of justice, it is guided by a higher commitment than simply winning a victory for one's own side. By definition, justice raises particular issues to be matters of public interest, not just private concern. Using justice as a frame of reference in public debate can safeguard activists from views and appeals that appear narrow and self-seeking.[5]

Although it is difficult and requires unusual discernment, defending the right of others to have space to believe and practice their distinctives is a principle of justice God invites us to follow.

Look for encounters with people who are different. Dealing with the diversity that swirls around us while keeping our integrity intact means also looking for ways to encounter people who are different from ourselves. Acquiring reliable knowledge about others and personally getting to know them will often alter the way we perceive those different from ourselves.

As theologian Hans Küng points out, religious practices illustrate that we have "spectacular differences from one another." For example, Christians know that Muslims and Buddhists have to abstain from alcohol in any form. Drinking alcohol in moderation is normal for some Christians, on the other hand, while others practice abstinence. Jews and Muslims know that Christians may eat pork, while Christians know that Jews and Muslims regard pork as unclean. Sikhs and strict Orthodox Jews may not cut their beard or hair, but Hindus, Christians and Muslims may keep their hair as short or as long as they wish. Christians may kill animals, while Buddhists may not.[6] Although we may disagree with certain practices, understanding the *reasons* different religions hold particular convictions can generate respect.

If learning about people can generate respect, getting to know people quite different from ourselves can be transforming. The value of understanding basic Islamic teachings pales in comparison to the impact of having a personal conversation with Omar and Shari, who live down the street. One may hold strong convictions about homosexual lifestyles or people who have had abortions, but listening to the struggle of Steve and the pain of Mary will touch us at a deeper level. Having had such personal encounters gives us the privilege of substituting names of real people for the rightness of our theoretical convictions. And to be touched with tenderness is to be more fully human.

Go beyond mere tolerance. On a scale of virtues, tolerance is much preferable to intolerance. Intolerance is harsh and cruel, judgmental and exclusionist. Tolerance acknowledges the rights of others and makes room for their views and values. Giving people the right to exist is still a bare minimum, however. When we just tolerate people, we inevitably send signals that we are merely putting up with them. Attitudes of toleration stop short of fully humanizing others.

Speaking about how Christians should view other faiths, former archbishop of Canterbury George Carey calls us to "friendship, not hostility; understanding, not ignorance; reciprocity, not exclusivism; and cooperation, not confrontation."[7] Religious studies professor Douglas Hall of McGill University reasons that tolerance is "simply looking past people, allowing them to have their beliefs, however 'false,' because we really don't care." It is not good enough, for the One said not "Tolerate your neighbor" but "Love your neighbor."[8]

While we are legally and socially required to tolerate people in our pluralistic society, in God's order of creation mere tolerance is not enough. God's way is to move beyond tolerance to acceptance and love.

PURSUING PRINCIPLED PLURALISM

Democratic societies that are both pluralistic and principled make room for all the citizens they contain. They create social structures to cradle their collective diversity. Political theorist Paul Marshall defines pluralism succinctly: "The basic notion of pluralism is simple: that there are in society different people with different beliefs and different ways of life and that they should as much as possible be free to live out their beliefs without being controlled by others."[9]

The tension that inevitably ensues for concerned Christians is how much freedom is good for society as a whole. The individual challenge is to resolve what it means to be true to one's personal commitments and religious tradition while still engaged in a pluralistic world.

Be who you are. One critical response in a pluralist world is to confirm our personal commitments and then carve out our cultural space. It is imperative that we give ourselves permission to be who we are and then be prepared to express the meaning of that identity in our private and public life.

In my private life, I am a follower of Jesus who believes many things, including certain principles about how God wants me to conduct myself sexually. My wife and I have had the privilege of a long-term relationship that has honored our covenants of sexual faithfulness. I'm not claiming sexual purity or denying the allure of sexual temptations, but I am committed to honor both God's call and my marriage vows. I believe God's ideal is that sexual intimacy be expressed in heterosexual family relationships of covenant and commitment. I am prepared to articulate and defend God's ideal both privately and publicly and seek ways to influence others to believe and live in the same way. While I take my stand, however, there are people who I know by name and care about who do not live by the same convictions: some choose to dishonor their marriage covenant, others cohabit without any intention of making a permanent commitment to each other, some decide to live in homosexual relationships.

There are various ways of responding; here's my attempt at faithfulness. On the betrayal and adultery front, I *lament and relate*. Broken promises and disobedience produce woundedness. Responding with lament and disappointment is more redemptive than projecting judgment. Regrettably, it is sometimes impossible to maintain relationships with all the parties involved in triangles of betrayal. But making phone calls and being present is preferable to silence and abandonment.

When cohabitation is the practice, my response is to *pray and relate*. Whether I approve of the practice is immaterial. Today's young people are delaying their transition from family dependence to patterns of independence and interdependence. The stage of romantic engagement is being replaced with cohabitation. Marriage is usually the long-term intention, but for many there will be various starts and stops along the way. Staying involved and praying that there will not be the deeper damage of abortions and unwanted children is better than pointing accusing fingers.

Where homosexual relations are the choice, my response is to *express regret but also relate and lobby*. My regret is that people who choose to live in homosexual relationships end up defining themselves by a focus on their sexual preference. They reduce their humanity down to a single dimension when there is much more potential for meaning and fulfillment. My desire is to lobby on two fronts. Because God's heterosexual ideal is better for both individuals and society at large, I support social policy initiatives that defend the historic definition of marriage. However—you may disagree with me here—because homosexual lifestyles do not contravene the contemporary criminal code, I'm supportive of all the human rights of homosexual people.

The strategy I suggest for learning to relate to sexual diversity and other manifestations of difference is quite straightforward:

- self-define and clarify your identity
- find socially appropriate ways to act on your commitments
- engage in the public dialogue while seeking to influence public policy
- leave room for the preferences of others who also have the democratic and God-given right to self-define

But along the way, seek to retain relationships. When relationships are broken off, the potential for ongoing involvement and redemptive influence is shattered.

Give permission to others to be who they choose to be. A basic element of principled pluralism is to extend the same privileges to others that we take for ourselves. For example, if we want to voice our views in the public forum, then others with differing views should have the same prerogative. The intent is not to permit just anything but to make room for attitudes and behaviors that do not violate either criminal codes or social decorum.

While living in a war-torn region of former Yugoslavia, Miroslav Volf shaped a deeply Christian response to the brutality raging around him. His example calls us to an even more profound level of responding to others. The will to give ourselves to others and welcome them, to readjust our identity to make space for them, is prior to any judgment about them beyond identifying them in their humanity. The will to embrace precedes any "truth" about others and any construction of their "justice." This will is absolutely indiscriminate and strictly immutable; it transcends the moral mapping of the social world into "good" and "evil."[10]

If we allow Volf's prophetic call to influence our attitudes and actions, we will stop limiting life for others to our own boundaries. Without groaning or whining, and whether we agree or not, we will surrender cultural space to the personal preferences of others.

Martin Marty poses a challenging question: "Is it possible that in this unfolding of human history there will be significant groups who can, without a sense of superiority, still project their truths and values among others, without manipulating them?"[11] For North Americans in particular, what are the obstacles for those who have economic, social and political power to be true to themselves while restraining their use of power so that others can self-define, make their choices and pursue their futures?

Treat people as God treats people. Living with a sense of superiority over other people breaks the rules of principled pluralism. People who aggressively assert that their ways are the right ways for everyone inevitably send the message "We are better than you are." People with such strong convictions are often deeply committed followers of Jesus. Yet when we look closely at Jesus' attitudes and actions, there is no trace of him projecting any sense of superiority over the people in his presence.

We will move toward creating the human history God hopes for when we treat people as God treats them. "God's reception of hostile humanity into divine communion is a model for how human beings should relate to the other."[12] Since the episode of disobedience in the Garden of Eden, God has acted to subdue evil and counter the damage of sin. God's interventions have repeatedly appealed to the rightness of truth and the power of love. Including Christ's death on the cross, God's truth has been spoken forth with conviction tempered with compassion, but the motivation has always been to restore relationships. When we make room for others who are different from us in the same way and with the same end in mind, we will be true to ourselves.

DIRECTION FOR THE JOURNEY

One of our shared human flaws is the tendency to self-size life—that is, to reduce life down to *my* size. And when the legitimacy of everyone's beliefs and behaviors is limited to our own views and personal preferences, we surrender to another enemy with a smiling face.

The tragedy for self-sized and culturally contained people is that they live isolated lives inside their self-imposed restricted space. Intellectually closed systems prohibit the possibilities of new ideas. Restricting social space to present boundaries precludes discovering the richness of new relationships. And downsizing spiritual space to my church or my personal style prevents the wind of the Spirit from blowing divine freshness into our tired human spirits.

"The task in front of us," urges journalist John Gray, "is to forge terms of peace among peoples separated by unalterably divergent histories, beliefs, and values."[13] My spirit reaches for a shared future when our children will inherit cultural space where people are so secure in their personal and social identity that they can deal nondivisively with others who are different from themselves.

Alongside St. Francis, we can courageously pray, "Grant that I may seek not so much to be right as to relate."

11 Balancing Conviction and Compassion

The news item on the radio left a series of dangling questions. The report sketched an incident between a sixty-two-year-old man and a city bus driver. The man boarded the bus with an outdated ticket that didn't include a recent ten-cent raise in the purchase price. Evidently the driver demanded the additional ten cents. An argument ensued over the unpaid portion of the fare, and according to the report, the passenger started physically beating the driver. It was only when some of the other passengers pinned him to the floor of the bus that the police were called and the man was carted off to jail. The man's name was not given, and no other specifics were detailed.

How do we respond when we hear about such incidents? Perhaps we think, *If anyone is that stupid, they should spend some time cooling off in jail.* Or maybe we are inclined to wonder, *What kind of pressure in a person's life would trigger such a drastic response to a request for ten cents?* Is our reflex response to assign blame, or do we wonder what caused such bizarre behavior? Anyway, why didn't somebody on the bus offer to pay the ten cents?

The intention in posing the questions is not to deem one response right in order to declare the other wrong. Rather, it is to acknowledge that people are wired for different styles. Some people instinctively read situations based on their convictions about what is legal, proper and right. They contend, "People have to live with the consequences of their actions. Unless we have strict social rules, life will become even more chaotic." Other people readily give compassionate responses. After all, it is reasonable to assume that something other than a ten-cent coin was the real reason for the man's anger. "Is it possible that the older man was fired from his job just before he would have retired? Or perhaps he had been picked up for drunk driving and was angry with himself for having to take the bus."

A equilibrium of conviction and compassion is critical to our shared future. Without conviction, our personal lives are permissive and without boundaries. Without compassion, we become harsh and judgmental. In the larger society, conviction without compassion produces social policies that press too hard on problem people—the unproductive people who "rip off" the system. Compassion without conviction, on the other hand, leads to systems that can reward deceit and foster behavior that lacks honor.

Even though virtues are profoundly important to our personal and social well-being, virtues also have vulnerabilities. Unchecked and unbalanced, virtues can become vices. If they function without the influence of each other, conviction and compassion become social and religious villains. They lead to excesses that open the door for enemies with smiling faces to enter and take up residence.

TRUTH-DRIVEN CONVICTION

Many North Americans are experiencing turbulence at the intersection of their private and public lives. At one extreme, some people are living with moral rage. They believe public life is betraying their private commitments. Liberalization on issues such as abortion, euthanasia, homosexuality and pornography marks the crumbling of society. At the other extreme, civil libertarians and people who tend to be permissive believe individual rights and freedoms need to be protected. They contend that issues relating to poverty, economic opportunity, progressive social policy and the role of government in these matters deserve much more attention than they receive. Politicians gladly pay for polls to help position themselves among the factions so that they can find favor with social issue voters.

People who get out of bed in the morning with the potential to express moral rage are most often energized by truth-driven conviction. Their sense of right and wrong is informed by something greater than simply their personal notions. They are truth people. They have got it right, and they are ready to let others know what is right.

In Christian terms, truth-driven people not only serve as defenders of the faith but also act as definers of what is right for others. Because they are theologically correct, they live with a sense of certainty—and that certainty fuels intensity. With the Bible as the source of their conviction, there is no other option than to declare what God has clearly revealed.

We need people with truth-driven conviction. Otherwise the spirit of the age can lull us into spineless, compromising permissiveness. Conviction is, after all, the building material for consciences that will not crumble under pressure. Informed conviction leads to discernment and an increased capacity to live with integrity. Life without conviction is limp and wimpy. However, as virtuous as truth-driven conviction may be, without the presence of compassion to counter its inherent force, conviction can be destructive. Conviction without compassion is an enemy with a smiling face.

A challenge of living in any society is deciding how to relate to those who are different from us. Whether it is by deliberate choice or the result of inevitable social segmentation, there is no escape from dealing with self-definition and what it means for relationships with others. The table "Relational Ethics" overviews the different ways our beliefs interact with our social style.[1]

Tribalizers' embrace of conviction is both a virtue and a vice. On the virtue side of the ledger, Tribalizers have backbones made of steel. They stand tall in their beliefs and are not easily swayed from the convictions they cherish. Tribalizers are committed to win at any cost and make superb defense lawyers.

Relational Ethics

	personal slogan	social style
Tribalizer	My ways are the only way.	Confronter
Reclaimer	My ways are the right ways.	Converter
Cocooner	I won't bother you with my ways, and don't bother me with your ways.	Retreater
Accommodator	Your ways are as good as my ways.	Includer
Collaborator	Let's create space for both our ways and let God work—that's the only way.	Cooperator

On the vice side of the ledger, Tribalizers are blinded by their biases and boundaries. They are "one eye and one ear" people. They are capable of seeing only what they see and hearing only their own voice or those that echo their convictions. They have genuine difficulty hearing or seeing life from the other's point of view. Consequently, they are comfortable with "us against them" encounters.

Those in the abortion debate who are adamantly either "prolife" or "prochoice" are taking a Tribalizer stance. There can be no middle ground. They are ready to isolate and segregate people and, if necessary, shred the fabric of society to get their way. Tribalizers do not understand that "moral indignation drives us to condemn others; conscience prompts us to question ourselves."[2]

Tribalizers rate extremely high on the virtue of conviction and extremely low on the virtue of compassion. They are unbalanced people. The Tribalizer slogan is "My ways are the only way." Their social style is to confront.

Reclaimers also display conviction as both a virtue and a vice. They stay true to their convictions, but unlike Tribalizers, they do not find it necessary to have emotional convulsions to do so. Still, Reclaimers can be counted on to resist any change that stands in opposition to their clearly stated principles.

Culturally, Reclaimers' slogan is "We were here first and you should be like us." They are among those who contend, "If I'm right and you don't agree with me, you must be wrong." Faced with challenges from the influx of other ethnic groups with their own cherished customs and different religions, Reclaimers appeal to their cultural seniority. Spiritually, Reclaimers genuinely believe that "my god is better than your god" and are sure you would be better off converting to their specific beliefs and resulting behaviors.

Reclaimers also tend to yearn for yesterday. Their view of a better future is a return to the "good old days" of the past. They remember a world before abortion was legal, when "family values" were assumed, when there was no easy access to pornography and when Sunday shopping was limited to the necessities. Their solidly grounded and deeply held convictions give Reclaimers an enormous capacity to be judgmental of others. Reclaimers are high on the virtue of conviction but low on the virtue of compassion. They are unbalanced people. Their social style is to convert others.

When conviction overwhelms compassion, "my ways" push aside the ways of others. Fuller Seminary president Richard Mouw reminds us that "there are many texts that apparently lean against judgment. Didn't Jesus himself tell us, 'Do not judge, so that you may not be judged'? And didn't our Lord show us what this means by his own example, accepting people just the way they were—including prostitutes and tax collectors, who were generally considered to be very undesirable types?"[3]

Frederick Buechner reflects on his days at Harvard Divinity School and remembers the pride of its style of pluralism—feminists, humanists, theists, liberation theologians all pursuing truth together. He realized then that "the danger of pluralism" arises when it becomes "factionalism, and that if factions grind their separate axes too vociferously, something mutual, precious, and human is in danger of being drowned out and lost."[4]

LOVE-DRIVEN COMPASSION

If truth-driven people have backbones of conviction, then love-driven people have hearts of compassion. They are the mercy people. And when they show up in our life, they are reminders of God's grace. Their sympathetic nature makes them more aware of complexity than of certainty, more inclined to accept ambiguity than to demand clarity. The hearts of compassionate people lean to the left. Because their mind is not already made up about everything, they find it relatively easy to make room for others and their differing views.

Love-driven compassion people are theologically empathic. They celebrate the merits of gracious orthodoxy. Belief is blessed without the requirement of getting it all right. The theology of compassionate people does require action, however. They believe that deeds of love done in the name of Christ put a human face on the God of creation and redemption. And the result is tangible benefits to single parents and high-risk children, to Aboriginal peoples, the unemployed and the underemployed. People trapped in addictions, those with a criminal record who want a fair chance to begin again, and children and adults with disabilities who have been sidelined get welcomed back into the mainstream.

Our world needs people with love-driven compassion. Otherwise we would be left with the aftermath of unchecked legalism and judgmental harshness. Compassion is more inclined to look for reasons life isn't working than to point fingers of blame at people deemed dysfunctional. Compassion looks for ways to redeem broken situations. Life without compassion is self-centered. And when we cannot feel with others, we are incomplete, and we become cold and indifferent.

Still, as virtuous as compassion may be, without the presence of conviction we become soft and sentimental. Blind acceptance is substituted for discernment; ambiguity is blessed as principled morality. Compassion alone can be destructive. Compassion without conviction is an enemy with a smiling face.

Accommodators have compassion as both a virtue and a vice. Their instinct is to see and appreciate the beauty of God's creation in almost everything. Accommodators celebrate the goodness of the human spirit and minimize the darkness of sin. Accordingly, the gifts of God as Creator overshadow the need to encounter Christ as Redeemer. If one must choose, the importance of love triumphs over the importance of truth.

God's love for Accommodators and their love for God motivates their concern for justice and the needs of others. When the rights of others get trampled, their conviction rises up. When Accommodators perceive that injustice marginalizes a minority group, they have the capacity to behave like Tribalizers. And they have little patience with people who warn that they could lose their soul to the dangers of syncretism.

Accommodators are in tune with social sensitivities. Being politically correct can be as important for them as being biblically correct. They prefer to reject being judgmental in favor of being inclusive. Accommodators welcome diversity and take pride in being early adopters of what is innovative and new. Their tendency to be cultural trendsetters means Accommodators run the risk of simply accepting the norms of the prevailing culture. Instead of prophetically bringing God's eternal ways "on earth as it is in heaven," they are vulnerable to being culturally assimilated. Accommodators are extremely high on the virtue of compassion but extremely low on the virtue of conviction. They are unbalanced people. The Accommodator slogan is "Your ways are just as good as my ways." Their social style is to include.

There is another sizable group: people who live without much concern for either conviction or compassion. They are *Cocooners*. Neither truth nor love frames their existence. The Cocooner disposition does not automatically make them bad or evil people. Cocooners are simply socially detached. They are happy to be left alone doing what they want to do. Cocooners tend to withdraw into their private space and disengage from issues that trouble others. They know how to program their VCR and DVD player so that they can do what they want with whom they want. They turn off the television and shut down the Internet to think about broader issues only when their personal interests are directly jeopardized. Whenever possible, personal convenience controls their behavior.

Cocooners look after themselves. They get out of bed in the morning, eat breakfast, send their kids to school, go to work, pay their taxes and make regular payments on their credit cards. In the summertime they exchange pleasantries with their neighbors as they cut their grass right up to the edge of their property line. They have little sense of responsibility for the people who live next door or down the hall. Cocooners are "live and let live" people who silently signal, "Let's stay out of each other's way."

Cocooners who attend church do so on their own terms. They worship more than they work. They do not serve on committees, and sacrificial giving is left to someone else. Cocooners are not extra-mile people. The absence of conviction keeps them out of politics and away from public demonstrations. The absence of compassion means Cocooners protect themselves from feeling other people's pain. They do not lament what they do not experience. Cocooners score low on both conviction and compassion. The Cocooner slogan is "I won't bother you with my ways and don't you bother me with your ways." Their social style is to retreat.

VIRTUE-DRIVEN BEHAVIOR

There are ditches on both sides of the road. Conviction and compassion are the guardrails that keep us from veering off the road and traveling in the ditch. Truth that nurtures conviction protects us from mindless permissiveness. Love that motivates compassion protects us from judgmental arrogance. Balancing conviction and compassion in our attitudes and behaviors brings together the virtues of truth and love. It is the coexistence and counterbalance of conviction and compassion that protects us from excesses that turn these virtues into vices.

Collaborators are people who embrace both the virtue of conviction and the virtue of compassion. They are neither permissive with themselves nor judgmental toward others. Collaborators live in the tension of seeking to influence others without either apologizing for their convictions or denigrating the convictions of others. They are committed to mutuality. Collaborators are "us" people. They collaborate, not to be in collusion like traitors but in order to cooperate with the people around them.

Although Collaborators are more inclined to include people than exclude them, they are not easily co-opted. They believe that truth exists to be discerned, and they are ready to draw lines between what they conclude is right and what is wrong. Collaborators know who they are and what they believe. They have limits and live within moral boundaries. Out of the clarity of their self-definition they resolve to be true to themselves and carve out personal and cultural space for their commitments.

Although compromise is not a dirty word for Collaborators, they are not ready to live contrary to their convictions.

Collaborators live by the code of extending the same privileges to others that they take for themselves. They are reciprocal people. They believe that win-win solutions can be discovered and negotiated. Besides finding enough cultural space for themselves, they desire to do the same for others.

Their conviction insists, *Be true to yourself,* but their compassion compels them to *live with regard for the rights and views of others.* For Collaborators no single sector of society has a right to rule over all. They know the sound of their own voice but reject the notion that one voice can speak for everyone.

Collaborators live out the theory articulated by faith development scholar James Fowler: "When the spine of identity is well established, it is possible to risk relating in depth to those who are different from self."[5] Collaborators rely on the strength of their self-definition to give them the freedom to accept others who think and behave differently. Whether the concerns to be resolved are moral, ethical, sexual, social or religious, the Collaborator spirit of mutuality convinces them that "together we can find a way." Collaborators are high on both conviction and compassion. They aim to balance these virtues. The Collaborator slogan is, "Let's create space for both our ways and let God work—that's the only way." Their social style is to cooperate.

A message on a birthday card that was sent my way captures the Collaborator spirit:

> Here's to the man who knows
>   who he is and where he stands,
> the man with enough confidence in his
>   own beliefs
> that he isn't afraid to let others
>   express theirs . . .

Although none of us limit our attitudes and lifestyles to only one of the above categories, each of us does have a particular style that will predict our most probable behavior. And we all need to find a balance between compassion and conviction.

As long as we reside on the earth side of heaven, even with God's help we will be less than we desire to be. Though I intentionally aim to practice the Collaborator creed and live that social style, too often I find myself feeling the attitudes and expressing the virtues and vices of the other styles. As long as God allows me to live, I will have to work at living with myself while responding to other people who are living their creed and expressing their style.

ADDRESSING RELIGIOUS DIFFERENCES

One of the ongoing challenges for me is being true to my Christian convictions while making room for other Christians who hold different convictions. Richard Lovelace clearly states what we know to be true: "Different groups within the Christian church are at odds with one another because their models of the Christian life, its beginnings and its fullness, are so diverse. . . . One person's piety is often another's poison."[6] Regrettably, the gospel is often locked in church structure prisons and the activity of the Spirit is confined to rigid theological systems.

God has obviously decided to allow different models of the Christian life to coexist and stay active in the midst of their disarray. Clearly, Catholic and Orthodox churches continue to write their sacred history; since the Reformation, the Protestant denominations are still parading their distinctives; Augustine, Calvin, Arminius and Wesley have their followers; and charismatic believers bring their particular flavor to the Christian family. The question for the moment is, how do the virtues of conviction and compassion affect how we respond to pervasive Christian differences?

An additional challenge for the balancing of conviction and compassion is the increasing cultural presence of other world religions. If we struggle to deal with *Christian* differences, how can we possibly address the chasms that separate what is essentially Christian from the tenets of the other world faiths? Do we look for common ground, identify our differences and invite dialogue, or build walls and isolate ourselves from their influence?

Pope John Paul II uses his positional authority and personal conviction to propose a response:

> The Catholic Church rejects nothing that is true and holy in these religions. The Church has a high regard for their conduct and way of life, for those precepts and doctrines which, although differing on many points from that which the Church believes and propounds, often reflect a ray of truth which enlightens all men. However, the Church proclaims, and is bound to proclaim that Christ is "the way and the truth and the life" (Jn 14:6), in whom men must find the fullness of religious life and in whom God has reconciled everything to Himself.[7]

The range of responses from Tribalizers to Accommodators reveals how the presence or absence of conviction and compassion affect how we understand and respond to both Christian and world religion differences.

Christian Tribalizers see the faith in right-and-wrong categories. You are either a member in good standing of my church tribe, endorsing my correct doctrines, or you are outside the Christian camp. Divergent views are not tolerated. Doubts are denied or held in silence. Living with a readiness to control and if necessary confront life around them, Tribalizers are often blind to what is sacred and important to others. They can be counted on to lobby and vote against zoning laws that would allow mosques or temples into their neighborhood.

Christian Reclaimers see the faith in black and white with some room for shades of gray. Members of the Christian family need to get it right when it comes to the gospel's core doctrines. Mainline Protestants can bless other mainline Protestants; evangelicals can accept other evangelicals; charismatics can celebrate with other charismatic believers. Lines are often drawn between Protestants and Catholics, or those who are born again and those who are not. The drive to convert others prevails. Convinced that their way is the true way to understand life, Christian Reclaimers commit themselves to convert members of other world religions to their particular view of faith. They readily pray and give financial support to the efforts of missionaries sent to foreign lands.

Christian Accommodators are more drawn to the Great Commandment to love than they are to the Great Commission to go and make disciples (Mt 22:36-40; 28:19-20). The assumption of God's goodness in all creation dulls any desire to evangelize and convert. Accommodators are generally content with the spiritual state of others. Motivated by compassion and concerned about not offending or judging anyone, Accommodators roll out the welcome mat to people, especially if it is rumored that they are subject to discrimination. Accommodators tend to embrace the premise that all religions are equally valid.

Christian Cocooners are content to find a church where they feel they belong. They are ready to fit in and stay settled if their personal and family needs are met. They are reticent to make commitments that would get them overinvolved. They stay at home when their church mobilizes people for outreach and service events. Cocooners are busy taking their children to dance lessons and basketball, football or hockey games. If they have no children, career development or their latest personal interest occupies their time. Cocooners are indifferent to multifaith issues unless an excessive number of visible minority people seem to be moving into their community.

Christian Collaborators affirm their spiritual self-definition and respect the spiritual self-definition of others. They perceive that the Christian life is offered in diverse packages but what is inside is often the same: newness of life in Christ. They believe the activity of God's Spirit transcends the human limits inherent in all church structures. They are ready to "speak the truth in love" inside the Christian family and in the world (Eph 4:15). Striving to affirm their own convictions while accepting the convictions of others, Collaborators look for common ground and seek to be bridge builders. Without reticence, they engage others about what they believe and seek to influence people to respond to Christ, but they do so with regard for what is important to others. While Collaborators resist the idea that all religions are equally valid, they are ready to make room in society for other religions and their practices.

Collaborators are advocates of life according to the Golden Rule. Their faith in God as the Creator of people everywhere propels them to believe that the Golden Rule travels two ways. Not only does God invite us to "do to others what you would have them do to you," but in the divine plan for human existence, we should expect people to treat us the way we treat them. The Collaborator disposition is consistent with the Arapaho proverb that counsels, "When we show respect for other living beings, they respond with respect for us."

An examination of the beliefs of the world's religions reveals a measure of shared commitment to the Golden Rule virtues of reciprocity and mutuality:

Christian. "In everything do to others what you would have them do to you; for this is the law and the prophets." (Mt 7:12)

Brahman. "This is the sum of duty: Do naught unto others which would cause you pain if done to you." (Mahabharata 5:1517)

Buddhist: "Hurt not others in ways that you yourself would find hurtful." (Udana-Varga 5:18)

Confucian. "Surely it is the maxim of loving-kindness: Do not unto others what you would not have done unto you." (Analects 15:23)

Taoist. "Regard your neighbor's gain as your own gain and your neighbor's loss as your own loss." (T'ai Shang Kan Ying P'ien)

Zoroastrian. "That nature alone is good which refrains from doing unto another whatsoever is not good for itself." (Dadistan-I-dinik 94:5)

Jewish. "What is hateful to you, do not to your fellow man. That is the entire Law; all the rest is commentary." (Talmud, Shabbat 31a)

Islamic. "No one of you is a believer until he desires for his brother that which he desires for himself." (Sunnah)

DIRECTION FOR THE JOURNEY

Whatever virtues we may name, when excesses take up residence in our lives there are two critical consequences. First, they impose undesirable restrictions on us. The virtues that are present in excess take up so much room that no space is left for other virtues. If conviction reigns in our attitudes and behavior, then the influence of compassion is thwarted. When compassion rules in excess, it denies the expression of conviction.

Second, unchecked excesses keep us from making room for the views and values of others. Our ways are so dominant that they block our understanding of and appreciation of other people's ways. We compulsively impose on others our self-sized conclusions about how life is to be conceived and lived. In doing so, we inevitably end up treating other people in ways that we do not like being treated. When we transgress the Golden Rule, we cannot relate in positive ways, and we forfeit the possibility of influencing others who are different.

Feminist writer Naomi Wolf proved a remarkable Collaborator as she spoke with vulnerability at a Common Ground conference in the 1990s.

> When you open yourself to the kinds of change that common ground creates, you lose aspects of your identity that you have been clinging to. I had parts of my ego stripped away from me. It's very humbling. I had to face the fact that I might have been wrong all this time, and that people I felt united with in solidarity might be wrong. The other painful thing I had to face was that I owed an apology. I needed to ask forgiveness for the wrong I had done.
>
> I'll remember for the rest of my life what happened when I apologized to the pro-life people in the room at a common-ground conference. I thought I would lose everything by asking for forgiveness and, of course—no surprise to you, big surprise to me—I gained a sense of freedom. I felt truly liberated in a way that all that us-them liberationist rhetoric I had labored under all my life had never freed me.[8]

Wolf's confession sets the standard for the rest of us who hold strong views. The redemptive attitude and response is "Grant that I may seek not so much to be right as to relate."

12 Dignifying Cultural Differences

Encounters with people are usually more powerful than interactions with ideas. When we know people by name, their presence and their experience is difficult to refute, let alone demean. Ideas are more abstract, more elusive and more vulnerable to our judgments and rejection.

I had an encounter with a man quite different from myself that still leaves me pondering. His name is Nathaniel. His family roots are in East Africa, and his skin color is deep black. We had a conversation one evening over a meal at a small table in Dakar, Senegal, in West Africa. Even today, when I close my eyes I can see the shape of the Island of Goree scrawled across the skyline just a few kilometers off the shoreline by that Dakar restaurant.

The Island of Goree has a renowned history. A tourist attraction, the island features architecture of a colonized history of Portuguese, Dutch and French conquerors. But the real historical story is that Goree was a slave-trade prison compound. It was one of the transit centers where black African captives were gathered and locked up until they were shipped off to the New World as commodities to serve the economic interests of plantation owners and other people with social power.

My supper companion was a gracious man, soft-spoken and gentle, insightful and eloquent. Nathaniel's personal gifts and life experience had made him wise. As our discussion took various turns, I kept seeing the Island of Goree out of the corner of my eye. I wondered if some of Nathaniel's ancestors had been held there on their way to the New World.

Because Nathaniel had lived much of his life in Muslim-majority regions, I asked him how he dealt with people who held different religious commitments from his own. He smiled, and our conversation suddenly deepened. Nathaniel talked about the criteria we use to validate and discredit other people. Himself a committed evangelical Christian, he told me that some of his Catholic friends had shown him some things that seemed to be missing from his Protestant beliefs and practices. He went on to talk about his years of working in poor communities alongside Muslims.

After listening to his story, I asked, "On this side of all those experiences, what memories bring you the most pleasure?"

Without a pause and with a beaming smile, he recounted the day some Muslim community leaders said to him, "You are the first Christian to show us that Christians love Muslims."

When we shift our focus from Dakar, Senegal, to Savannah, Georgia, we do more than just travel across the Atlantic Ocean. We connect the events of history and see how we are shaped by where we are born and what we are conditioned to assume. I was walking the streets of Savannah a few weeks after my experience in Dakar and was struck by the long, painful effects of the legacy of the past. In modern Savannah, hotel managers are white and service staff are African American. Business owners are white and cashiers are African American. The wealthy are white, and most often the poor people are African American. Tourists are invited to tour plantations to see how life used to be, but it is all too evident that the class structure of the past continues to reign.

As I write this chapter, both Oprah Winfrey and Tiger Woods are cultural icons. Oprah Winfrey is black and proud of it. Tiger Woods's father is African American and his mother is Thai. Even though Winfrey's and Woods's skin color is dark, they have towering social prominence and influence. Still, African Americans and other citizens who share dark skin colors are often subject to discrimination and are ghettoized in urban centers and disadvantaged neighborhoods.

Why do we sometimes think we are better than other people—that people with one color of skin are superior to those of another color? In our age of enlightenment, why do some people suffer discrimination and face social obstacles because they belong to a minority group? When we are tempted to rank others according to their similarity to our own likeness, we are guilty of self-sizing. Further, it is a warning sign when we stay silent and passive while others created in the image of God are subject to social stigma and cultural prejudice. It is evidence that enemies with smiling faces have moved in and taken up residence.

COMMON ROOTS

Those of us who live in North America are all boat people—boat people in two different ways. Our first voyage goes all the way back to Noah. Claiming his Aboriginal descent, pastor Dan Doolittle explains, "I've always encouraged people to go back to Genesis. We're all boat people. We all got off the same boat. Through Noah we all came from the same bloodline. God doesn't see any differences in us. We may have different color skin, but we don't need racial barriers or any other barriers between us."[1]

Our second voyage is linked to our family roots. With the exception of Native Americans, we North Americans are all immigrants. Our own families may have been present for more generations than some others. Sadly, some of our ancestors arrived as slaves. But we share common immigrant roots because at some time in history we all came from somewhere else. Our ancestors crossed an ocean and started a new family story. Whether we can trace all the family connections is not the issue. We all find our roots in families that disembarked from a boat—or in more recent time, that exited from an airplane.

Many of our ancestors arrived on the continent with a definite agenda for their future. They wanted more freedom and opportunity than their past had allowed them. Freedom to choose one's religious expression was particularly high on the list for immigrants to the United States. What may not have been understood in the beginning is that a culture of freedom of choice generates an explosion of differences over time. The differences are not just racial, religious, ethnic and linguistic. Increasingly, the distinctions involve social class, lifestyle preferences, diverse ethical perspectives and the assumption of sexual prerogatives. As multicultural advocate Neil Bissoondath asserts, "A free society depends on a multiplicity of voices and visions, on the interplay of conflicting views." At this point in history, he says, "we would only diminish ourselves by diminishing that variety."[2]

The inevitable question for "free choice cultures" is, how much diversity is too much? When does freedom of individual choice transgress the collective well-being of others in our shared cultural space? The historic precedents established by both civil and criminal law set limits on our behavior. Our cultural rituals and social codes also act as deterrents to off-limit behaviors. But because both laws and rituals are evolutionary by nature and life itself continually generates new scenarios for us to deal with, tensions over how to live peaceably and productively with each other will be present until the end of time.

Assuming that choices are inherent in our modern pluralistic culture, sociologist Peter L. Berger helpfully observes that pluralism is not just "a lot of people of different colors, languages, religions, and lifestyles bumping into each other and somehow coming to terms under conditions of civic peace. Pluralism also impinges on human consciousness, on what takes place within our minds."[3]

In the inner sanctum of our mind and in the shelter of our private attitudes, how do we really feel about people whose customs are different from our own, whose food sometimes smells offensive, whose language is foreign to our ears and whose music can sound like the dragging of a sharp object across a blackboard? Do we look for escape routes, feel intrigued enough to stay around and develop a relationship, or secretly think, *Why don't you go back to where you came from?*

Missionary Miriam Adeney warns against regarding plurality as a bad or bewildering thing. "I like to think of God's glorious multicultural kaleidoscope. I view cultures as treasure chests of symbols for exuberant expression of the image of God. It's true that people as sinners create patterns of idolatry and exploitation in every culture. Equally, however, people in God's image create patterns of beauty, wisdom, and kindness in every culture."[4]

CULTURAL CONTAINMENT

One coping mechanism many people employ for dealing with multicultural diversity is to retreat into cultural containment and become ethnocentric.

We all need places to belong. We become emotionally fatigued when the life we share with others lacks common reference points. We need people around us who don't require long explanations in order to understand what we mean when we speak. When we belong, our acceptance is not conditional on our performance, and we don't have to get everything right all the time.

However, such closeness to the groups where we belong creates other complications. Being surrounded by sameness is like living in a world without color. It nurtures bland uniformity, excessive agreement and mind-numbing boredom. Instead of creativity, conformity is required. Innovation is unwelcome, and fitting in is necessary if one is to remain in good standing with the group.

Having lived in the midst of ethnic and religious conflict in the Balkans, Miroslav Volf offers a strong word of counsel to counter such homogeneity in our Christian church cultures:

> In order to keep our allegiance to Jesus Christ pure, we need to nurture commitment to the multicultural community of Christian churches. We need to see ourselves and our own understanding of God's future with the eyes of Christians from other cultures, listen to voices of Christians from other cultures so as to make sure that the voice of our culture has not drowned out the voice of Jesus Christ.[5]

Volf's perceptions are especially germane for citizens of the United States, given the absence of checks and balances to the present power of their government on the global stage.

While excessive sameness dulls life, Stephen Kliewer points out the danger of excessive diversity in group life. It results in a loss of focus, he says. When a group has "too much diversity there are not enough common beliefs and goals upon which to base the group's existence, motivation and direction. The 'glue' is missing and the energy expended simply to hold the fragments of the group in close proximity to one another robs the group of any power to act."[6]

Participating in group life that permits a balance between being an insider who belongs and relating to others who belong somewhere else will protect us from the shriveling effects of self-sizing ethnocentrism.

LOYALTY CHOICES

Although it is seldom stated overtly, multicultural societies implicitly appeal to multilevel allegiances. Each element in the cultural mix of ethnic identity, national patriotism and religious faithfulness invites a particular loyalty. And the demands of the three realms are certain to conflict with each other with some regularity.

In *Blood and Belonging* Michael Ignatieff defines "civic nationalism." He paints a picture of a nation "composed of all those—regardless of race, colour, creed, gender, language, or ethnicity—who subscribe to the nation's political creed." Such nationalism is called civic "because it envisages the nations as a community of equal, rights bearing citizens, united in patriotic attachment to a shared set of political practices and values."[7]

National loyalty is a social consequence of healthy civic nationalism based on common citizenship and a healthy measure of patriotism. According to the civic nationalist creed, what holds a society together is not common religious or ethnic roots but the role of law, the shared values of civil society and a bias toward national self-interest.

In the same book Ignatieff goes on to define "ethnic nationalism." Here, in contrast to civic nationalism with its binding together through shared citizenship and patriotism, the dominant ethnic people group both defines and holds the society together. In its extreme form, ethnicity demands nonnegotiable allegiance: trust only those of your own bloodline, and give blind loyalty to each other within that group. "This is how ethnic cleansing began to acquire its logic. If you can't trust your neighbours, drive them out. If you can't live among them, live only among your own."[8]

Religious loyalty is a pervasive force in North American culture. Preaching and teaching from church pulpits have shaped the social ethics and personal values of our nations. The virtues of the Christian faith have created what is best about our national conscience and collective commitments. But at the same time, the Christian faith has been used by some as an instrument of divisiveness and judgment.

Advocates of either side of the abortion debate have used the issue as a justification to insult, demean and even kill each other. Christian believers bent on "religious cleansing" have carried placards around church parking lots while funerals honoring the lives of homosexuals were taking place. Convinced of their righteous rights, people have invoked God's good name to deny law-abiding citizens their human rights. Too often churches have condoned racism and other forms of injustice with their silence. Too often those who are saved by grace have not extended grace to others. Too often blind religious loyalty has downsized the views of the faithful into expressions of faith that betray the faith.

Whether the focus of commitment is ethnic, national or religious, indiscriminate loyalty can be lethal. Too often the interplay of national, ethnic and religious loyalties has torn apart societies and left people alienated from each other.

Forces of ethnic nationalism tyrannized the lives of millions of people during World War II. A shared Christian faith was not strong enough to stop the Hutu and Tutsi tribes from killing each other in Rwanda. In former Yugoslavia, the Croats, Serbs and Albanians continue to translate their ethnic, national and religious loyalties into hate and destruction. Northern Ireland's history is a litany of death justified in the name of ethnic and religious loyalty. Palestinians and Israelis flaunt their evil acts of destruction as badges of honor and belonging to their tribe. In the United States, a major part of the populace goes to prayer in support of the deployment of military troops sent to wreak havoc on another part of God's creation. Will we have to wait until Jesus returns before the horror ends?

Theologian Craig Van Gelder still believes that the Christian faith can lift us above the rule of ethnic or national self-interest. He contends that the people of God can be "formed around a different identity, one that transcends race, ethnicity, and nationalism. It will be an identity rooted in a shared faith and fellowship with the living God. This new community will include people of diverse racial, ethnic, national, and political identities."[9] In the midst of pervasive evil and excessive brokenness, our best hope is to pray and discern, to reject what destroys and embrace what restores justice and brings peace.

MULTICULTURAL PRACTICES

Discerning and taking on respectful multicultural practices in our everyday life can move us closer to what God has in mind for our coexistence on planet earth.

Assume the equality of human worth. If there is a touchstone for the human race, it is to stand on level ground with every other person on the face of the earth and declare: "God is the Creator of the whole world, and regardless of race, gender, religion or social status, every human being is created in the image of God and has equal worth."

Dallas Willard accentuates the point: "It is now generally agreed in this country [the U.S.] that differences of sex, race or religion, for example, are not inherently moral differences." A Hindu is not "better or worse, as a human being, than a Christian or Muslim, nor is a woman better or worse than a man. It is therefore wrong to treat the one as if he (or she) were somehow more deserving or more to be favored than the other."[10]

Acknowledge historic inequities. Male domination has characterized Western cultures. Glass ceilings have restrained the advancement of gifted women in the business world. Theological debates have turned a blind eye to spiritual gifting and closed the doors on the ordination of women. An entrenched cultural bias has kept women in kitchens and out of the political arena.

Whether the victims are ethnic groups or members of other world faiths, stereotyping and restricting people is often a consequence of social conditioning and personal ignorance. Canada's Aboriginal peoples—who struggle with enormous needs and a plethora of dysfunctional behaviors—are the recipients of both bias and ignorance that translate into expressions of injustice. It's true that suicide rates are high and education levels are low. It's a fact that alcoholism is rampant and dependence on social welfare is more the norm than the exception. However, it is also true that as a group these people were isolated on reserves that marginalized them. Their land was taken without adequate compensation, and treatment as second-class citizens has nurtured people who too often have second-class self-images. Until we acknowledge historical inequities and understand the systemic reasons for symptomatic behavior in marginalized peoples, we will continue to see with biased eyes.

A few days ago I heard Jayakumar Christian from India reflect on his experience at airports. His question emerged out of his personal experience: "If second-stage security checks are on a random basis, why am I selected for extraordinary scrutiny nine times out of ten?" If we are white and not subject to social profiling at security checkpoints, we may not recognize the issue. But if our skin is dark or our appearance suggests Arab descent, the experience can be embittering. Over time, historic inequities have a propensity to reappear. Are we aware? Do we care?

Accept and appreciate differences. In North America, dandelions are considered to be weeds rather than attractive flowers. In Korean culture the reverse is true: dandelions are valued and appreciated for their beauty. Korean American Jung Young Lee reflects that living as a member of a minority group is like growing up in the corner of a yard of beautifully mowed green grass as an unwanted dandelion.[11]

While our nations have policies recognizing cultural and racial diversity, formal policies do not control our attitudes. Rather, how we view people affects how we feel toward them. As long as we presume that our personally preferred ways are better than other people's ways, it will be almost impossible to affirm the validity of their ways. It is only when we accept the legitimacy of other people's perspectives though different from our own that we will be able to appreciate them. We will make advances in relationship with others who are different from ourselves only when we live out the Golden Rule and treat others as we would like to be treated.

Say no to all forms of denigration. It is impossible for multicultural practices to become social norms as long as we cling to old notions of ethnic superiority. And it is offensive and unacceptable to live in a society where it is permissible for one ethnic or religious group to implicitly or explicitly insult another group.

Over the years I have spoken to hundreds of diverse Christian and secular audiences. I have made a commitment not to make negative pronouncements about other organizations in any public forum. Sometimes I disagree strongly with the theological views, methodologies and practices of organizations different from my own. My approach, however, has been to define my own views and express those as persuasively as possible without demeaning the views of others. Those who find it necessary to put down others in order to establish their own positions are weak people who deserve pity more than respect.

Extend equal rights to all faiths. One of the paradoxes of modern life is that the Christian majority in North America's population sometimes feels as if it is subject to discrimination. It is felt that born-at-home faiths are subject to criticism and restriction of expression while recently arrived faiths enjoy the luxury of unscrutinized acceptance. In a recent court ruling, Canadian justice Kenneth MacKenzie concluded that "a religiously informed conscience should not be accorded any privilege, but neither should it be placed under a disability."[12]

Reflecting broadly on the role of religion in society, Harvard law professor Alan Dershowitz rightly contends that

> the world must be made safe and secure for disbelievers. America was founded on religious dissent and skepticism. We must not accept religious hegemony or preference for religion in public life. Atheists and agnostics are every bit as American, every bit as

moral, and every bit as qualified to hold public office as people are
who believe in an intervening God. Disbelievers should not accept
second-class status in a nation whose traditions and laws forbid
tests of faith as a condition of citizenship or office holding.[13]

A robust and healthy multicultural society will be marked with equal
rights for people of all faiths, including those who place their faith in the
premise that religious faith is futile.

Pursue justice for all. With few exceptions, claims Stan Gaede, "multiculturalism is not argued today on the basis of promoting justice but on
the grounds of inclusiveness. The fundamental assumption is that it is
good to be tolerant of different ideas and different perspectives. In other
words, undergirding current thought on multiculturalism is not some
sense of what is ultimately just and true."[14]

Gaede's gift to the discussion of multicultural superiority is to lift the
issue to its proper level. Respecting people and giving them a proper
place in social structures is not about being nice to them or tolerating
their uniqueness, it is about doing what is right. It is about pursuing justice for all.

The practical tension in both public and private life is to restore justice without inflicting more injustice. For example, some people contend that affirmative action practices in the workplace favor minorities
at the expense of the majority. In some cases that may be true. But when
historical inequities exist, the principle of justice for all requires decision-makers to wrestle with doing what is right. And doing what is socially right is far more complicated than dealing with just one individual.

Persevere in friendships. Unless we have friendships with people who
are ethnically, socially and religiously different from ourselves, we will
be tempted to treat multicultural issues only as theoretical ideas. But
when we care for people, enjoy them and name them as friends, the issues are no longer just ideas. They are about the experiences of people
we cherish. Multicultural practices in everyday situations constitute
learned behavior. Multiethnic friendships are crucibles for an acceler-
ated learning curve.

DIRECTION FOR THE JOURNEY

During the 1980s our family attended a Baptist church that was trying to figure out how to follow Jesus as a multicultural congregation. We were a collection of Caribbeans, Asians and white folk who worshiped and worked together. One of our active members was Theophilus, a native of Jamaica. He worked as a janitor, and when you shook his hand it felt like fine sandpaper. Theophilus always greeted you with a fabulous smile. Another person who participated regularly in the church was an eminent New Testament scholar. Dick was white, born in America, always approachable and engaging.

One Sunday morning I was worshiping near the front of the sanctuary and preparing to receive Communion. I was sitting in the pew next to the aisle, and when I turned to my left, Theophilus served me the bread with the words "The body of Christ." As I turned to my right and passed the bread to my wife, my eyes briefly made contact with the server in the aisle at the other end of the pew. It was Dick. For me, in that moment, "the body of Christ" leveled the ground we all walk on in a new way.

The Scriptures declare that in Christ "there is no longer Jew or Greek, there is no longer slave or free, there is no longer male and female; for all of you are one in Christ Jesus" (Gal 3:28). With God's help, and when the reign of Christ is "on earth as it is in heaven," ethnic superiority dissolves, social discrimination dissipates, and gender relationships are transformed.

Grant that I may seek not so much to be right as to relate.

13 Global Citizenship

Life shrinks. Left to find its own way, life tends to close in on itself. Maybe it's a gravitational pull built into the human temperament, or maybe it's the physical law of entropy, but it is almost inevitable that what is closer to self-interest pushes aside what has less self-interest. The pattern is predictable at both macro and micro levels. National priorities preempt global concerns. State and provincial preferences overrule national and federal interests. Local community issues are somehow more important than regional matters. The needs of my family really are more critical than the well-being of my neighbor's family. And if a choice has to be made between my aspirations and a competitor's, I prefer receiving the benefit.

There are exceptions, of course, but life tends to shrink. Unless we resist the drift toward shriveling self-interest, life will downsize to our self-size. Ethnocentrism will take up residence, and yet another enemy with a smiling face will embrace us.

GLOBALIZATION IS UNSTOPPABLE
The paradox in these times is that even though self-interest is rampant, increasing globalization is unstoppable. Even if all the presidents, prime

ministers and dictators in the world gathered and unanimously agreed to put a stop to globalization, they would not be any more successful than if they decided to control the wind. The ascendancy of technology and flow of information, economic connectedness and environmental inter-dependence, the desire for self-determination and the assumed right to make choices, the movement of peoples and insatiable aspirations for higher standards of living all blow through our borderless world. Some-times in some places the winds feel like a gentle cool breeze on a hot night, and other times they appear like tornados wreaking havoc.

Thomas L. Friedman, author of *The Lexus and the Olive Tree,* reasons that this new system has its own unique logic, rules, pressures and in-centives and deserves its own name: *globalization.* Globalization is not a passing trend. It is the dominant international system that has replaced the Cold War system since the fall of the Berlin Wall.[1]

The media fan global winds. Television beams its signals everywhere. Once a World Vision staff colleague was telling of her experience in a re-mote rural area of Bangladesh. In a village where some people did not know whether they would have something to eat on any given morning, people gathered to ooh and ah at the glamour of the beautiful-people party at the Academy Awards.

TVs and VCRs with their music and movies are global delivery sys-tems. They transmit their beats and rhythms, messages and propaganda into the entire world. Noted economist John Kenneth Galbraith states flatly that television has become "the prime instrument for the manage-ment of consumer demand."[2] And how can we possibly imagine the im-pact of cyberspace? The Net with its ocean of data and images, knowing no borders except the barrier of economic poverty, will enter every na-tion and keep leveling our global ground.

There are two nagging questions that persists in our present world with its international imbalance of cultural and military power: Is there any real difference between globalization and Americanization? And if the spread of America's influence is as inevitable as globalization, is this desirable or undesirable?

Joseph Epstein exposes a cultural vulnerability of pro-Americans:

"Americans have felt themselves, if not quite a chosen people, then at least living in a chosen country, enjoying God's special blessing."[3] Yet from the perspective of those who live elsewhere and embrace other world religions, the ways of the West are sources of the godless spirits of secularism and materialism. Rather than evidence of God's blessing, the individual permissiveness and insatiable appetite for affluence that mark the West are interpreted as evidence of God's absence from American culture.

Within hours of the horrendous collapse of the Twin Towers, media commentators and people in hallway discussions were exclaiming, "The world will never be the same." And there is an element of truth in that statement. However, there is more than one perspective to the tragedy. A Kenyan who had endured the attack on the American embassy in Nairobi a year earlier responded simply, "Welcome to the world." September 11, 2001, will go down in the historical records for many reasons, but perhaps rather than just interpreting the event as an act of terrorism we will also understand the day as a *globalization of suffering*.

Regardless of how we choose to piece together the flow of interaction and influence in the world, globalization is unstoppable.

INEQUITY REIGNS

The global reality is that some people suffer far more than others. Lifetime advocate for the poor Ron Sider explains: "At a time when there is plenty of food, we still have about 800 million people undernourished. The World Bank reports that approximately 1.2 billion people must try to survive on less than a dollar a day, and that 3 billion people must try to survive on less than $2 a day."[4] The three richest officers of Microsoft, Bill Gates, Paul Allen and Steve Ballmer, have more assets, nearly $140 billion, than the combined gross national product (GNP) of the forty-three least-developed countries and their 600 million people.[5]

"In the next 20 years," asks Michael Novak, "what will the 3 billion people whose average income is $2 a day or less conclude when they are informed about how wealthy people live? What will the poor conclude about the indifferent moral quality of our generation's Christians—and our generation of human beings?"[6] If the circumstances were reversed and we were struggling to survive, how do you think we would view the rich?

These troubling issues are not restricted to countries whose GNP leaves them outside the economic elite. Sider notes that "in the United States, the richest nation in human history, about 34 million Americans live in poverty; about 44 million have no health insurance."[7]

"When I eat Mexican food in the evening, jog the calories off the next morning in Vietnamese-made Nikes, and then on Sunday see a missionary video of Tanzanian children with swooshes on their shirts, I am living globalization."[8] Our lives are intertwined with those of the world's poor. Theologian Hervé Carrier challenges all our consciences: "Who will provide the modern world with hope in view of such agonizing questions about our common future?"[9] If those of us who claim to be followers of Jesus do not hear the cries of the poor and lead the charge to challenge local and global inequity, who will?

I must confess that issues of global inequity fade when I am at home watching television or having supper on my backyard deck. Living in a country that collectively pays for access to universal medical care, I am also emotionally distanced from the vulnerability of uninsured Americans who simply can't afford to get sick. Still, even though I cannot single-handedly reorder these global inequities, my lack of empathy for those who exist daily without the basics of life dehumanizes all the world's citizens. So I need reminders to keep thinking, praying, giving and acting with compassion. Recently I heard an African mother's prayer that made me feel the pain inflicted by global indifference: "I pray for the children who want to go to school today but don't have clothes to wear and money to pay the fees. . . . Many of them have bright minds; it's such a waste. God, please bring people to care for them."

Jim Wallis, editor of *Sojourners*, reminds us that "despite the many noises of this society that distract our attention, assault our minds, and harden our hearts, we have a very real stake in one another's lives. And the circumstances of the most vulnerable among us are always the best test of our human solidarity with one another."[10]

GLOBAL CITIZENSHIP

Global inequity is never going to go away completely. Some countries are blessed with a wealth of natural resources, while others are virtual wastelands. Every country brings its unique history into the twenty-first century, and sometimes that legacy is more of a liability than an asset. Dreaming and working for global equity seems impossible in places where tribal peoples are continually at war with each other, where floods, famine and typhoons wreak their havoc over and over again, and where cultural and religious practices deny basic human freedoms. Canada is not Cambodia, England is not Ethiopia, the United States is not Armenia. "Location, location, location" is not just a real estate agent's chant; it is a predictor of both undeserved affluence and undeserved poverty.

Vaclav Havel, former president of the Czech Republic, helps us grasp some dimensions of our global reality. "Globalization by itself is morally neutral," Havel contends, adding: "It just is. It can be good or bad, depending on the kind of content we give to it. It's up to us to use globalization for meaningful purposes, not for nonsense.

"For instance," he says, "the interlinking of people and the spread of information and capital can be either good or bad." As a "good," he cites the spread of information about human rights, how to defend them and who violates them. As a "negative," he cites the spread of silly sitcoms or even stupider commercials, which give a false picture of life.[11]

Although globalization itself is morally neutral, living in a country with a standard of living that soars above the poverty that grinds people down to subsistence levels elsewhere does raise moral issues. Do people living in comparative affluence have a moral obligation to curtail their privileges in order to share with others? Does geographical distance justify moral distancing and abdication of responsibility for others who live elsewhere?

Once I walked down a hallway of a government building conversing with a wealthy, socially powerful woman who was also a committed Christian. She asked, "What do you want me to do? Move to a smaller house, downscale my wardrobe, turn in my theater tickets and give my money away to the poor?"

Our friendship allowed me to smile and jest, "That would be a good start." Then we had a more serious conversation that centered on the challenge we both face to live responsibly and appropriately in our own culture while still relating and responding to people in other cultures.

Just as an encounter with Christ does not annul one's temperament and personality, disciples of Jesus are not extracted from the culture they live in. Although there are times when biblical faithfulness means being countercultural, Christians are not deculturalized people, expected to alienate themselves from their social context. Rather, an encounter with Christ energizes people to inject Christ's influence into the societies and neighborhoods where they work and live. Life in Christ brings the possibility of choreographing life with coherence—including giving compassionate responses to people living near us as well as in other parts of God's world.

EXAMINING ATTITUDES

The attitudes we carry around inside us are like positioning devices. They are the impulses that trigger our actions and reactions. Unexamined attitudes leave us responding to stimuli and reacting to perceptions in the same old ways. When we have the courage to probe our inner self, we encounter the potential to alter our attitudes. We can cultivate attitudes that encourage us to live as if we carry two passports, nurture expectations of mutual learning and alert us to practices that exclude people. They can also position us to respond to people who are less fortunate than ourselves.

Carry two passports. Unless we are refugees looking for a welcoming place to call home, we all have the privilege of carrying a national passport. We have a national identity. We belong somewhere. My Canadian passport gives me a nationality that allows travel and entry into the territory of other nations.

But as a person created in the image of the Creator God, I also have another identity. God's world is my world, and my citizenship extends beyond my nation's borders. I am a global citizen and carry two passports. I have something in common with every other human being. "The rich and the poor have this in common: the LORD is the maker of them all" (Prov 22:2).

My global citizenship entails both privileges and responsibilities. When the attitude I carry inside is based on two passports, my national interests cross borders into international territories, and I am pressed to perceive and respond to the world's events accordingly.

Mutual learning. The principles of working with people in poverty-stricken communities include the assumptions that everyone has something to contribute and everyone involved should expect to learn from each other. Know-it-all attitudes violate the spirit of mutual learning. In contrast, relating to others with the expectation that their experiences and perspectives will enhance my own lifts life to new levels.

Some laws of life are universal. When mutual learning is an anticipated norm, whether people are poor or rich, old or young, they feel valued and are motivated to express their opinions and make their unique contributions.

Resist exclusion. Community development practitioner and poverty theorist Jayakumar Christian points to the *exclusion* of the poor as one of the primary reasons for their predicament. Len Doyal and Ian Gough conclude that, "This exclusion of the poor is rooted in the world's rejection of the wisdom of the poor as not worthy of any attention." In the attitudes of the rich, the voices of the poor are regarded as "damaged goods," blemished by ignorance and inferiority.[12] The regrettable consequence, contends Robert Chambers, is that "the poor exclude themselves by not participating in social and political processes. The poor do not speak up; they may even decline to sit down with the powerful. Weak, powerless and isolated, they are often reluctant to push themselves forward."[13]

The attitude and tendency to exclude is not just a long-distance issue. Street people are rarely consulted in the development of social policy intended to improve their lot. Church members on welfare are seldom expected to make contributions to the framing of outreach strategies focused on their community. School dropouts are not often considered valuable resources for the creation of "stay in school" programs. Unless the natural human inclination is countered, the bias of the healthy is to exclude the unhealthy. The disposition of the strong is to discount the value of the weak. We can do better.

Safeguard dignity. Secular and Christian organizations that exist to respond to the needs of the poor are governed by and monitored according to codes of conduct. For example, when the pain and predicaments of the poor are publicized, those in need are to be portrayed as "dignified human beings, not objects of pity." Paternalistic messages are off limits, and cultural respect is the standard. Degrading and demeaning images breach the ethical code. The intent of the regulations is to guard against dignity destroyers.

Jayakumar Christian identifies another practice to avoid. "Years of work among the poor have taught us that limiting our investment among the poor to just money makes the poor beggars, and limiting our investment to programs makes the poor glorified beggars."[14]

The need to safeguard the dignity of people who live with poverty also applies to how we respond to those who work the streetcorners of cities in North America and other continents. When my schedule takes me into the inner city and I'm alert enough to plan ahead, I go to my stash of change and put two or three dollars in my pocket. Then when I'm faced with a street person holding out a cup or lifting up a scrawled sign, I'm prepared to respond. After many experiences of passing a little money to people begging and feeling uneasy about the exchange, I'm now working on the dignity issue. Instead of passing by quickly pretending I don't really see the person, I stop, reach into my pocket, look the person in the eye and say, "I hope you have a good day, and God bless." Most often the response is "God bless you too."

Some critics argue, "Street people are professional beggars. What they need to do is find a job. All you are doing is encouraging their exploitation." In some cases that may be true. But I suspect that if we could hear the stories of street people, whether they practice their craft in North America or Africa or Asia, there are reasons they live as marginalized people. And in the human drama where some of us are more blessed than others, preserving human dignity is more important than being exploited for a few dollars here and there.

DIRECTION FOR THE JOURNEY

The following story has been told many times, and it deserves to be retold.

A man spoke with the Lord about heaven and hell. The Lord said to the man, "Come, I will show you hell." They entered a room where a group of people sat around a huge pot of stew. Everyone was desperate and starving. Each held a spoon that reached the pot, but the spoon had a handle so much longer than their arm that it could not be used to get the stew into their mouth. The suffering was terrible.

"Come, now I will show you heaven," the Lord said after a while. They entered another room, identical to the first—the pot of stew, the group of people, the long-handled spoons. But here everyone was happy and well-nourished.

"I don't understand," said the man. "Why are they happy here when they were miserable in the other room and everything was the same?"

The Lord smiled. "Ah, it is simple," he said. "Here they have learned to feed each other."

The city of Mitrovica, Kosovo, is a divided city. Among its population of 100,000, Serbs live on one side of the river and Albanians stake out their territory on the other side. Ironically, 90 percent of the total population is Muslim.

During the height of the civil war that inflicted ruin on the city, World Vision was able to deliver massive amounts of goods and services to help the people cope with the deprivation of war and the conditions of a harsh winter. The challenge was how to distribute the needed humanitarian aid fairly. A decision was made to gather the religious leaders and seek their counsel. Then a resolve was reached quickly. Even though the vast majority of the population was Islamic, the Muslim imams requested that the supplies be distributed so that Serbian Orthodox Christians received a third, Roman Catholics received a third and Muslims received a third.

As we learn to respond to the predicaments of our global neighbors, God's kingdom will come "on earth as it is in heaven." Along the way, the spirit of St. Francis's prayer will help us see and feel life from the point of view of the rest of the world.

Grant that I may seek not so much to be right as to relate.

14 Global Engagement

Tensions exist for those of us who take our faith seriously and wrestle honestly with living globally. We wonder about living rich alongside appalling poverty. We are uneasy about accumulating more and more when many live with less and less. Because of the enormous political and economic power of the West, we struggle with the consequences of our foreign policies and the protectionist trade embargos placed on people living in the world's poorer nations. And when we take time to reflect, we know we could be doing much more to alleviate the suffering of those in the Two-Thirds World. How can we release some of our tensions and create more opportunities for others who live on our shared planet?

One option, of course, is to do nothing. We can restrict the focus of our days and nights to our immediate concerns and personal interests. The other option is to expand our vista beyond our home boundaries and escape the enemy of global indifference. It is to move beyond global indifference to global engagement.

But if we choose to participate in our globally connected world, it will be important to affirm a set of global core values and practices: moral, ethical, spiritual, social and economic principles for making planet earth truly human.

GLOBAL ENGAGEMENT

I can't get the picture out of my mind. As a member of a small group of World Vision staff, I visited Rakai, the high prevalence HIV/AIDS area in southern Uganda. Our host introduced us to Rachel. She sat in front of her little hut with her three children, ages seven, five and three. Her husband had recently died of AIDS. We had been informed that Rachel was also HIV positive and in the latter stages of AIDS. The medication that might have helped prolong her life was too expensive and hard to obtain.

After listening to Rachel's fears for her children, contrary to our common practice, my colleagues and I emptied our pockets of Ugandan currency and gave it to our host, saying, "Try to take care of the children." Thinking about my own three blessed grandchildren and struggling to imagine what would happen to Rachel's soon-to-be-orphaned children, I walked away and wept.

Become informed. We naturally perceive reality through the windows that are closest to us. It is unfair to have any other expectation for ourselves or for others. We make sense of life from the inputs we receive and the immediate frames of reference that inform our views. It is no wonder that when we hear about the HIV/AIDS crisis in Africa and other far-off regions that we instinctively think about homosexual lifestyles, drug users, dirty needles and the occasional victim of infected blood. Regrettably, our nearby windows are not adequate looking glasses for showing us the struggles of those beyond our borders.

In Africa and throughout Asia, the HIV/AIDS pandemic is a global crisis that will make earthquakes and tornados look like modest intrusions. The effects in the lives of innocent victims are staggering. Babies are born to die prematurely. Sexually faithful wives are victims of their husband's sexual unfaithfulness. Children are required to become heads of household; sisters and brothers are forced to function as sole caregivers and decision-makers. Desperation leads to the sexual trafficking of young girls. Instead of retiring and receiving the care of their children, grandparents are starting over again as mothers and fathers to their grandchildren. A longstanding myth is that if you discover you are HIV positive, all you need to do is sleep with a virgin and you will be cured. Thus the victimization spreads.

Although HIV/AIDS is a worldwide plague, in Africa alone forty million individuals are HIV positive. Fourteen million orphans already face a tenuous and confused future. The capacity and resources of extended families and concerned volunteers are almost exhausted. The implications of the infected and affected defy our comprehension, but those who strive to survive face inescapable pain. North Americans who look out their stay-at-home cultural window and assume homosexual lifestyles and drug use as the explanation for the catastrophe are looking through a glass darkly.

Ignorance may be the excuse, but indifference and disregard for the pain of others are tragic consequences. Hans Küng calls on us urgently: "We need people in all continents who make themselves better informed and orientated about the people of other lands and cultures, who take up the impulses of other religions and at the same time deepen the understanding and practice of their own religion."[1]

Defend human rights—everywhere. Human rights are not about doing what we want, when we want, where we want, with whom we want. Human rights are about creating a planet where people have what is necessary to survive with dignity—that is, with food available for adequate meals; with a roof to cover one's head at night; with education and basic healthcare within reasonable reach of mothers, fathers and their children; with opportunities to work in order to live responsibly; with protection from crime, sexual abuse and arbitrary arrest; with the right to participate in political process and cultural life; with freedom to think, speak, worship and seek one's God-given potential. In other words, the quest for human rights is much more about needs than about wants. Human rights give assurance to people that they can live with a future tense.

On the occasion of accepting his Nobel Peace Prize, Kofi Annan, secretary general of the United Nations, asserted, "I believe the mission of the United Nations will be defined by a new, more profound awareness of the sanctity and dignity of every human life, regardless of race or religion."[2]

In democratic countries as well as in nations governed under other systems, it is usually marginalized people who risk losing their rights and their dignity. The unemployed, the poor, sexual nonconformists, single-parent families, street people and refugees often need others to come to their defense.

Share the wealth. "When the waterhole gets smaller, the animals get meaner," states an African proverb. Conversely, is it also possible that when countries get wealthier, their citizens get greedier?

Bill Gates is one of the wealthiest men in the world and is often subject to judgments, but greed does not rule his life. The evidence resides in the twenty-four-billion-dollar Bill and Melinda Gates Foundation, the world's largest philanthropic foundation. Speaking with the integrity of his generosity, the chairman of Microsoft Corporation called for a campaign of voters who say, "I'd like to vote for politicians who think about global equity."[3]

Gates has a political ally in Senator Patrick Leahy. Noting a projected increase of $120 billion in the annual spending commitment, totaling $450 billion for the U.S. military in the next five years, the senator challenged all Americans, "For God's sake, show some humanity if you are going to be the wealthiest nation on earth. You have a moral duty to do something, and we are not doing it."[4]

Neither the Gateses' billions nor the government's commitment of tax dollars addresses the issue of sharing the wealth as individuals. At the very least we can allocate a percentage of our overall giving to the needs of the poor who live beyond our national borders. After all, generosity in our greed-nurtured culture is a modern Christian distinction. Brian McLaren says it plainly: "We live in the most affluent culture in the most affluent period of human history. If we can't discipline ourselves to learn the joys of generous living, I think we're an embarrassment to the gospel."[5] Beyond expressing our Christian conviction and compassion, giving globally is evidence that we carry two passports, one for our national identity and one as a citizen of God's world.

Pray for peace. John Gray states what's obvious: "The task in front of us is to forge terms of peace among peoples separated by unalterably divergent histories, beliefs, and values."[6] But as right as the global task may be, most people often feel helpless and hopeless. We feel that Israeli-Palestinian hate runs too deep, Christian-Muslim violence in Indonesia is too distant, and war through recent decades in the Sudan and Angola has produced an intractable way of life.

Prayer may be our only expression of hope. So we pray to the God of creation and redemption. We pray for warlords and presidents, for the guilty and the innocent, for those who wield influence and those who are weak. We pray that people will wake up tired of wanting to kill their enemies, that they will reawaken their conscience and desire peace. We pray for the politically powerful who can allocate funds to create conditions that promote peace and redress injustice. We pray that women will be protected from abuse and that their voices will be welcomed with the respect they deserve. We keep praying, "On earth as it is in heaven."

COLLECTIVE ACTION

Individual responses to people in poverty allow us to address our personal responsibilities and make peace with our conscience. Individual responses alone, however, will not be adequate to address the systemic creators and perpetuators of poverty.

Do no harm. The expression "Do no harm" is used by medical doctors seeking to avoid any harmful interventions, but it is also a principle that applies more broadly. At a global level, the distribution of food aid can do harm. It can result in lower prices at neighborhood markets. The dumping of surplus clothing so a company can receive a tax receipt can silence the sewing machines that provide the only source of income for women struggling to feed their fatherless families. The distribution of free Bibles and Christian books by well-intentioned Christians can put local bookstores out of business.

Child labor is a blight on God's creation that can cripple the long-term well-being of girls and boys. The efforts of lobbyists and advocates to decrease child labor and increase opportunities for children to go to school is noble and right. However, when families need the income from the work of their children in order to survive, child labor may be a necessary evil. Advocacy without alternatives can be shortsighted and harmful.

There is another "do no harm" pitfall to avoid. Whenever well-intentioned compassion creates long-term dependency, people have not been well served. Charity that turns people into satisfied welfare recipients instead of empowering them to pursue their independence is not a gift. Good intentions alone are not good enough. Discernment is needed—"do no harm."

Advocate for justice. Pursuing justice and addressing systemic causes of injustice and poverty are primary biblical concerns. The topics of justice and righteousness are addressed two hundred times in the New Testament and six hundred times in the Old Testament. Matthew records Jesus' indictment of the scribes and Pharisees for neglecting "the weightier matters of the law: justice and mercy and faith. It is these you ought to have practiced" (Mt 23:23). In Proverbs God's people are instructed to "speak out for those who cannot speak, for the rights of all the destitute. Speak out, judge righteously, defend the rights of the poor and needy" (Prov 31:8-9). The prophet Isaiah calls for specific action: "Seek justice, rescue the oppressed, defend the orphan, plead for the widow" (Is 1:17).

Sometimes we feel that national social priorities are in competition with international assistance programs. We reason that we have to choose, and taking care of ourselves must come first. But lobbying for the cancellation of crushing debts and for other measures of poverty reduction for the most impoverished nations does not jeopardize welfare at home. Purchasing coffee from a cooperative so that farmers in the Two-Thirds World can receive a fair share of profits may be inconvenient, but it does not affect our government's spending priorities.

It is morally right to boycott companies that manufacture their goods offshore and pay their employees slave-labor wages. Financially supporting reputable advocacy organizations that can influence decisionmakers at the World Bank and the International Monetary Fund toward framing economic policies that favor indebted nations is prudent Christian stewardship. Expressing strong dissent when government policymakers refuse to end the manufacture and sale of landmines is simply humane. Wondering why the lives of people in Afghanistan, Rwanda or Iraq seem to be less valuable than the lives of people in New York and Washington is evidence of godly discernment. Asking why six million people in Israel receive more U.S. foreign aid dollars than the multiple millions in sub-Saharan Africa and Latin America (with the exception of Colombia) combined is not just a matter of critiquing foreign policy, it is an expression of global citizenship.[7] Questioning longstanding trade sanctions that cause many children to suffer is faithful discipleship. Instead of quietly letting economic interests have the final word, mobilizing interest groups to champion environmental priorities is an expression of compassion on behalf of future generations worldwide.

Voting for politicians whose world is limited to their local and national interests ignores God's concern for people who suffer the multidimensional pains of poverty. An active concern for justice is not a Christian extra. Seeking justice on behalf of the marginalized is evidence of global citizenship and a biblical basic of Christian commitment.

Give children the right to hope. The life of the poor is marked by an absence of choices. When young children don't have the choice to go to school or to even think about what vocation may fit their interests and gifts, they may not be able to name their predicament, but they are victims of their poverty. Children who grow up eking out an existence can only conclude that life is more about survival than about having a chance to achieve their God-given potential.

With his voice trembling during the delivery of a Christmas message, Pope John Paul II made a plea on behalf of children: "Today, my thoughts go to all the children of the world: so many, too many are the children condemned from birth to suffer through no fault of their own. . . . Let us save the children, in order to save the hope of humanity."[8]

Children are born in innocence. They have no control over who their parents are, their birthplace, their citizenship, their social and economic status or the scope of opportunities that will come their way. They can be born privileged, or they can be born destined to a life with meager choices. Child advocate Fraser Mustard contends that civilized societies are defined by how people treat each other's children. And the mark of a civilized global *world* is how people who live with abundance treat other people's children who live without human rights or opportunities to be what God created them to become.

CHAMPION A VISION OF TRANSFORMATION

Bryant Myers, longtime leader in World Vision and author of *Walking with the Poor,* uses the term *transformational development* to reflect a concern for seeking positive change in the whole of human life, materially, socially and spiritually.[9]

Social stability. Living without social stability is like trying to cross the street at a multilane intersection without traffic lights. It's difficult, exhausting and dangerous. Political and police corruption, bribery in the justice system, inadequate access to education and healthcare, meager welfare systems and censoring of the press all contribute to social disarray. But the most devastating social ill is the torment of war.

The vast majority of the world's wars in the last fifty years have been internal civil conflicts. Within sovereign country contexts, people have been at war with themselves. However, for various reasons, in some cases the atrocities have precipitated a global response.

A writer for the globally minded *New York Times* observed the current trend: "What is the world to make of the new doctrine it thought was emerging . . . a doctrine, after Bosnia and Kosovo and East Timor—where the bulk of the world intervenes in countries that abuse their own citizens. . . . Large parts of the world, it seemed, were embracing the idea that universal standards of human rights were putting at least some limits on sovereignty."[10]

Placing limits on sovereignty can be an expression of responsible global citizenship. Whatever our views may be about building global coalitions to confront the abuse of single nations, one matter is certain: there can be no sustainable human transformation without social stability.

Economic feasibility. Achieving economic justice, Ron Sider suggests, "does not require equality of income or equality of wealth. But it does require equality of opportunity, up to the point where everyone has genuine access to the capital needed to enjoy a decent life."[11] Regardless of where people live, economic feasibility is one of the essentials of a humane world.

One of the initiatives making it possible for people to care for themselves in responsible ways is microenterprise development. Small loan banks are making capital available for people to set up their own small businesses and putting loan sharks out of business. The loans may be as little as fifty, one hundred or three hundred dollars, but they allow dependable and gifted people to pursue their dreams.

Microenterprise development with access to modest amounts of capital has enabled communities in Thailand to establish fish farming, organic fertilizer production and banana chip manufacturing businesses. The increased household incomes mean that parents put their children to bed at night with a proper sense of pride. In Uganda, families earn enough money in their woodworking and furniture-making businesses to buy better food and keep their children healthy. Women in Nicaragua used the profits from their pottery businesses to put cement floors in their houses, which has reduced illness in their children.

Loans to farmers in Romania enabled them to buy seed that produced higher-yield crops, which means they have enough income to pay their children's school costs. Access to low-interest credit has permitted poor people in Tanzania to transport their crops to commercial markets. Microfinance programs in Sri Lankan villages have enabled hardworking people to establish a juice-making business. They now live with self-respect and celebrate the privilege of employing others in steady jobs.

Some critics contend that economic development initiatives with the poor create more materialists, which is hardly what the world needs. We all know that money has the power to entice people to worship at the altar of materialism. While it is true that we do not have to be rich to be materialistic, it is also true that going without enough of the world's material blessings is not what God wants for anyone. It is tragic and unjust when people are forced to scavenge for scraps of food in garbage dumps. And surely no one is so hardhearted that they would deny parents the dignity of caring for the needs of their children. There can be no human decency—no sustainable human transformation—when opportunities for economic feasibility are unavailable.

Spiritual vitality. The privilege of interacting with and being influenced by people outside my own culture has reconfigured my sense of God's ways and what it really means to be a committed follower of Jesus.

Once, after a long day of interacting with malnourished children and listening to the laments of tearful mothers and anxious fathers, a colleague turned to me and said, "God is in the meanest of afflictions." I wanted to quietly say, "I'm not sure my faith is that strong."

In a moment of reflection another colleague once remarked, "I'd like to live so that I could get a Ph.D. from God." This prompted me to wonder what my vision is for my spiritual attainment.

Such affirmations of confidence in the Creator and desires to center life on the living God invade my spirit. They make me want to be more than I have been. Sometimes they reveal my Western spirituality to be form without substance. They disrupt my unstated longing for contentment. They lift my hopes of what faith in Christ can become. The deep-rootedness and aspiring goodness of the faith of others continues to compel me to believe there is more to be discovered.

It is no secret that where Jesus lived and the Christian church began is no longer the center of Christian spiritual vitality. The declining moral authority of churches in Europe is also a regrettable but an undeniable fact. Many who critique the church in North America point out that, although church attendance remains high there, the cultural influence of the church is meager. There are justifiable reasons for serious Christians in North America to lament.

Missiologists in the developing world have another view. They believe that once again Christianity will be saved for the world by its diffusion across cultural lines. The most striking feature of Christianity at the beginning of the third millennium is that it is predominantly a non-Western religion. Edinburgh professor Andrew Walls says all current data indicate that "the numbers of inhabitants of Europe and North America who profess the faith are declining, as they have been for some time, while the churches of the other continents continue to grow."[12]

Missiologists are now referring to "the coming of the third church." The first thousand years of church history were under the aegis of the Eastern Church, in the eastern half of the Roman Empire; the second millennium, the leading church was the Western Church. But in the third millennium the church will be led by the Third Church, the Southern Church—the church in the Two-Thirds World.[13] Samuel Escobar reflects, "There is an element of mystery when the dynamism of mission does not come from above, from the expansive power of a superior civilization, but from below, from the little ones, those that do not have the abundance of material, financial, or technical resources, but are open to the prompting of the Spirit."[14]

Our sense of our North American prominence in the world may be affronted by these spiritual projections. Still, where there is spiritual vitality, we have reason to celebrate God's presence. And as global Christians we will agree that wherever we live in the world, there can be no human transformation without spiritual vitality.

The faithful voice of John Howard Yoder contends, "The church's calling is to be the conscience and the servant within human society.[15] Hans Küng also believes that religions can have "liberating effects, orientated on the future and beneficial to human beings, and indeed often have had. They can disseminate trust in life, generosity, tolerance, solidarity, creativity and social commitment, and can encourage spiritual renewal, social reforms and world peace."[16] Clearly, the active expression of Christ's presence in the world's churches can transform cultures for the good.

Relational respect. Bryant Myers laments, "We may forget that the poor are not an abstraction but rather a group of human beings who have names, who are made in the image of God, whose hairs are numbered, and for whom Jesus died."[17] Jayakumar Christian pushes the line of logic to its natural conclusion: "Essentially, poverty is about relationships. It is a flesh-and-blood experience of a people within their day-to-day relationships. Within these relationships, the poor experience deprivation, powerlessness, physical isolation, and economic poverty."[18] When people are victimized by social structures that do not work for their wellbeing, instead of being empowered, they are debilitated.[19] The grind of poverty dehumanizes those who have been created to express their gifts and contribute to their families and their society.

Affirming the image of God in people trapped in poverty means treating people with relational respect. It is to celebrate their uniqueness and equality as members of the global community. Instead of expecting less and demeaning people, it is to stand side by side on level ground and negotiate agreements without any hint of superiority or paternalism. However we construct the relationships between those who are materially prosperous and those who struggle to exist, there is a global law: there can be no transformation without relational respect.

The majority of people who live in the northern lake zone of Tanzania embrace, and are embraced by, traditional animistic religion. Believing in the powers of witchcraft, they naturally blame untimely deaths and other evils on the spells of witches. Tragically, older women with red "witchcraft eyes" can then be hunted down and killed.

Without that understanding, my colleague's recent briefing would have been nonsense. With a proper sense of pride, Priscilla observed that a significant change in the community in the past five years was that older women with red eyes were no longer being killed. Her explanation made total sense. "Well first of all, because we now have an accessible health center, infant mortality is more an exception than an expectation. But there are other reasons. The impact of our Christian witness is twofold. We are telling people in the community the truth about why children die. It has nothing to do with the spells of witches. And more important, increasing numbers of people are becoming Christians, and churches not only are growing but are spreading the truth about God's ways."

Priscilla continued, "There is also another piece in the development puzzle. We live in a drought area here, and we are introducing drought-resistant crops and methods of productive agriculture. Farmers are growing different crops and producing much higher yields. The result is that the people trust us and appreciate us for what is happening. Our future hope is to take on issues like child rights, early marriages and other gender concerns."

Sustainable and transformational development is holistic. Instead of chaos and confusion about matters of life and death, social stability is established. Economic viability becomes feasible and sustainable. Spiritual truth replaces aberration, and relational bridges are built between people who hold shared hopes for their families and communities.

DIRECTION FOR THE JOURNEY

"The God of the Bible," notes Jim Wallis, "is the deliverer of the poor. This God has a special love for the disenfranchised and the marginalized—those who are on the bottom of everyone else's priority list."[20]

How else can we view God's ways? Christ invites us to become part of God's vision for a new earth, as articulated by the prophet Isaiah (Is 65:17-25):

- no dead children (infant mortality eliminated)
- maximum life span (access to quality healthcare guaranteed)
- build houses and dwell in them (shelter and security for everyone)
- plant crops and eat their fruit (employment and social stability)
- enjoy the work of your hands (economic justice assured)
- poverty eliminated (civil participation and fair distribution of resources)
- the wolf and the lamb will eat together (peaceful coexistence and mutual respect between people)

Isaiah's vision is stuff that dreams are made of. We can be cynical and opt for global indifference, casting aside the vision since "it's only possible in heaven," or we can resolve to reach up and pull down a little more of heaven on earth for all God's creation. One of the first steps will be to look beyond our national borders and respond to the grim realities endured by other global citizens, praying, "Grant that I may seek not so much to be right as to relate."

PART 4

STRATEGIES FOR LIVING
AMONG THE ENEMIES

*Grant that I may seek not so much
to outwit as to outlove.*

We cannot learn to deal effectively with enemies with smiling faces in just a weekend. They are too creative to be intercepted with conventional warning systems. They are too pervasive to be brought under control through moments of insight. Enemies with smiling faces are seductive; they are like shiny, red, poisonous apples. They appear with promise and potential, turn on us when we least expect it and inflict bewildering pain. Still, they are so attractive and compelling that we let them take up residence. Predictably, the enemies make promises they cannot keep. Consequently, we are left confessing our vulnerabilities and expressing our regret.

Followers of Jesus are especially vulnerable to the disappointment and hurt that the enemies inflict. Our desire to not just believe but also excel spiritually can propel us onto their paths of pain. But why shouldn't our confidence in the Christian faith lift our expectations? After all, we have the Scriptures to inform us, educated clergy to teach us, trusted friends to influence us and church communities to protect us. Yet the enemies intrude, deceive and deal out their damage. We end up feeling as if we've been betrayed in a love affair gone sour. We are left living in the ruins of broken promises.

Why didn't someone warn us that quick-fix faith is a short-term experience incapable of sustaining long-term results? We did not set out to become spiritually superior to others, but in our desire to be right, there was no option left but to deem others wrong. Someone should have protected us from our well-intentioned desires to believe while neglecting to develop our capacity to discern.

Classifying people who have little or no regard for God as "nonbelievers" or "non-Christians" is a common Christian practice. From a Christian vantage point, those who believe in Jesus are the "believers," and those who don't believe in Jesus are left with no alternative but to be the "nonbelievers." But Christian people are also supposed to believe in the value of all people. Why are we allowed to label other people in ways that divide us from them? Instead of meeting people for the first time and relating to them as they are, we classify people spiritually, which invites stereotyping and the projection of preconceived assumptions. The practice becomes an enemy that precludes and destroys relationships.

How have I been so blind? How have we been so blind? It's obvious now that everyone who breathes believes *something*. Why do so many followers of Jesus first want people to understand them, rather than seeking first to understand others? Part of being godly is holding to strong convictions. But the prospect of my conviction's becoming so strong as to make compassion a victim of excess offends my spirit. I'm tired of judging people. For God's sake, let me learn more about people who self-construct, who build their lives out of values and experiences different from mine.

When did our drive to be right overwhelm our desire to simply relate to people? How could we be so blind to the rights of others, so indifferent to global needs? I wish someone had shown me a long time ago that godliness in our day involves balancing conviction and compassion. Thank God, our world does not have to be self-sized down to our small-minded preferences.

The good news is that we do not need to keep living in the ruins. We can live among enemies without being victims of their cunning ways. We can find our way. The question remains, what strategies can help us live among enemies with a sense of poise and direction?

This last section invites us to join in the spiritual journey of the Great Commandment that celebrates self care, soul care and social care.

On the journey we aspire to pray and seek not so much to outwit people as to outlove them. The aim is not to be clever and cunning. Neither is it to outmaneuver people. Rather, with God's help, it is to think clearly, feel deeply, speak truthfully, love extravagantly and serve creatively. It is to live so that the faith has credibility, which helps to show that our faith is both plausible and believable.

15 Self Care

Nurturing a Mature Spine of Identity

The search for a satisfied self, a self with a coherent identity, is a sacred quest. The journey climbs the hills of *Who am I?* and visits the valleys of *Why am I less than I want to be?* The quest encompasses what we think about God and what we think God thinks about us. When our family roots bring us comfort and strength, where we were born is where we want to belong. Sometimes our feelings about our roots drive us to sever them, and we go searching for other places to call home.

I suspect that being fully alive means the search never ends. Certainly there are days and even weeks when our own integrity allows us the satisfaction of a quiet soul. But inevitably unresolved questions remain, insecurities return, and our souls become unsettled again. To be alive is to be unfinished.

Peter Berger's assessment is that people today are "afflicted with a permanent identity crisis, a condition conducive to considerable nervousness."[1] Although Berger overstates the case, we should not be surprised that twenty-first-century people "will not only be in search of meaning and community; they will also be in search of some anchor, some solid point of reference from which they can answer the question: 'Who am I?'"[2]

Christian teaching has not always helped to quiet the nervousness of our identity scramble. While it has been immensely reassuring to hear that we are created in the image of God, it has been destabilizing to be relentlessly reminded that we are unworthy sinners, unable to do anything in our own strength. I am not attempting to deny my sinfulness. Confessing that I have sinned "by what I have done and by what I have left undone" keeps me connected to our forgiving and life-restoring God. What I am resisting is pious but unreflective self-depreciation done in Christ's good name.

Being created in the image of God endows every human being with both inherent value and potential capacity to do what is right and good (Gen 1:26). Regrettably, sin and bad choices mar that ability to live as God first intended. Still, the Scriptures counsel us to embrace a balanced view of self: "I say to everyone among you not to think of yourself more highly than you ought to think, but to think with sober judgment, each according to the measure of faith that God has assigned" (Rom 12:3). In other words, we are to make a realistic, measured estimate of our human abilities. The Scriptures also teach that the gifts of the Spirit are treasures in God's people (1 Cor 2:12), treasures that do not evaporate every time we sin or fail to do what is righteous and honorable. And according to Jesus, the greatest command is to love—to love God with our whole selves, to love our neighbors and to love ourselves (Lk 10:25-28).

God's invitations to love include a call for *self care*. As we live among enemies with smiling faces, intentional care for ourselves is indispensable to holistic health and spiritual well-being. Self care is not the same as selfishness. It is not living in a closed universe bounded by me, myself and I. Rather, self care is knowing and accepting who I am, dealing with my strengths and vulnerabilities, giving myself permission to properly appreciate my human worth and living with appropriate self-regard. If we take Jesus' teaching seriously, self care is being able to look in the mirror and comfortably say, "God is doing something good here. I love God. I'm doing what I can to love the people in my life, and I love myself."

GETTING IN TOUCH WITH YOURSELF

The book of Genesis portrays Adam as the first identity consultant. He gave names to "all cattle, and to the birds of the air, and to every animal of the field" (Gen 2:20). Etymology is not my field of specialization, but I do know that names give meaning. Calling a bird "an eagle," for example, creates images and meaning; in the same way, the names we carry for a lifetime get filled with our personality, experiences and reputation.

An experience in India a few years ago helped to consolidate my identity in a new way. The sun had set several hours earlier, and I was out walking the streets of Chennai (formerly Madras). The sounds were foreign to my ears. The language was unintelligible to me; rhythms of music and an incessant beeping of horns formed a chorus of dissonance. The sights were intriguing. Cows wandered the city streets rummaging for food, storefronts were different from anything I'd ever seen, people wore garments quite different from mine. When I looked at the skin color and physical size of the people around me, it became clear: *This is not my home. I have friends whom I cherish and admire who live here, but these people are different from me. I don't belong here.*

My experience in Poland was quite different. As I wandered the streets of Warsaw, although the language was unintelligible to me, the sounds and sights were within my emotional reach. I began thinking about where my grandfather might have lived as a child, why he arrived in North America as an orphan, and why my father never taught me Polish. On my way back to the hotel, after I bought a CD of Fréderic Chopin's music, something happened. I looked at the other men on the street, noting their bearded faces, manual-worker northern European broad shoulders and Western social manners, and my spirit responded. *These are my kind of people,* I thought. *I could belong here.*

Regardless of the color of our skin or the language we speak, getting in touch with our ethnic and cultural roots is an important part of claiming our identity. Until we are able to find some reasons to celebrate our roots, our freedom to find our future self will be curtailed. We will be caught between our historical self and our current would-be autonomous self. If we fail to connect these two dimensions of ourselves, we will be left with a sense of incompleteness.

LIGHTENING THE BACKPACK

No one's background is perfect. Poor or rich, uncivilized or cultured, female or male, high school dropout or trailing a string of degrees, we all turn the corner from adolescence to adulthood with backpacks crammed with debris. The promise of our personal Garden of Eden is littered with good intentions that didn't work out and bad intentions that inflicted scars.

Every person's history is unique. There is only one you and there is only one me. We weave the fabric of our life with patterns and designs that are ours alone. We are shaped by the place and time of our birth, the genes of our parents, the formation and faith of our family, the influences of our culture, the scope of our opportunities, the consequences of our choices. Your story is your story and my story is my story.

I will never fully understand all the reasons my early concepts of God were quite distorted. Call me a slow learner, but it wasn't until I came into my mid-twenties that the fog about God's intentions for me began to lift. In my earlier years I saw God as a roving policeman. I might get by with my misdemeanors for a while, but eventually I'd hear sirens and be pulled over to receive my punishment. Instead of a lover who desired my good, God was a moral enforcer. Rather than envisioning God as a healer and enabler, I believed my lot in life was to conform and obey or suffer the consequences. I was afraid of God. I was afraid I would mess up and go to hell.

My disposition doesn't keep me dwelling on the past, but there is a childhood memory that helps me understand my confusion. When I was ten, I had an eleven-year-old Japanese friend named Jimmy. We went to school together during the week and attended the same church on Sunday. Jimmy loved baseball. In the small community where we lived, Jimmy's dad worked for the owner of a car dealership who also sponsored a semi-professional baseball team. One of Jimmy's delights was to be the bat boy for the team—which of course played its games on Sunday. The church we attended taught that "to remember the sabbath and keep it holy" included "no Sunday baseball."

One Sunday night I was at home and heard horrible news. That afternoon as Jimmy was enjoying his duties as bat boy, a stray foul ball struck him on the side of the head. Within a couple of hours Jimmy had died.

It was my first anguished encounter with death. I went to the funeral with my parents. As we came home, I thought of how I would miss my friend—and Jimmy had gone to hell.

The next Sunday at our small church, people were talking about Jimmy. Doubtless most were remembering Jimmy's good points and lamenting his loss, but one statement remains etched deep in my inner being. The woman who made the pronouncement was a good mother who loved her children and was faithful to her husband. She was a pillar of the church. Decades later I can close my eyes and hear her voice utter the words, "If Jimmy had remembered to keep the sabbath day holy, he would still be alive."

Coming out of my darkness regarding God's intentions took a long time. There are too many strands in the weaving to unravel here, but one much more redemptive memory bears retelling. I was studying the Ten Commandments when God gave me a revelation. For the first time, without reservations or qualifications, I suddenly grasped the good news that God's "big ten" were laws of love. What I had understood to be restrictive controls requiring fearful obedience were really invitations from a loving God who has good intentions for every person on planet earth.

I'm not suggesting my altered understanding of God means there are actually no negative consequences for disregarding the commandments. But when the source of the divine declarations is a wise and loving heavenly Father instead of a moral enforcer, the motivation for obedience is turned upside down.

My backpack is lighter than it used to be. It's still not empty. As long as God keeps granting me a little more insight along the way, I expect there will be other revelations allowing me to let go of more of the weight that still burdens me.

KEEPING SELF IN CHECK

Why is it that when I drive into a shopping center or arrive at the office, I look for a parking place closest to the entrance? I'm healthy enough to walk that extra distance, and I enjoy walking. I do not have to rush to punch in at a particular time. Honesty compels me to confess that when I arrive at my destination, I am thinking about what will be most convenient for me. The idea of parking in a remote area so that others can have the closer spaces doesn't enter my consciousness. Although my faith explicitly calls me to "do unto others" what I desire for myself, many of the routines of my life are marked by "me first" behaviors.

What else should we expect? The North American bias is to keep self at the center of the universe. We get swamped with "indulge yourself" invitations. The psychology of the age champions the need for "self-realization" as a precursor to "self-actualization." The book market parades self-help techniques. Church consultant gurus link future growth to the design of needs-based programs. Television shows image after image promoting the virtue of "doing unto yourself" whatever your self desires. As Paul Vitz incisively claims,

> We live in a time that is obsessed with the self. Self-worship may well be a perennial problem. It may indeed be the essence of sin and therefore nothing new. What is new about the current state of affairs is the fact that no other age has justified narcissism so enthusiastically. No other society has been so breathtakingly blunt in rejecting self-denial as a means to spiritual health and embraced the celebration of self as the highest good in the cosmos.[3]

Pastoral theologian Eugene Peterson injects sanity into our self-saturated situations. "People who pray know what most around them either don't know or choose to ignore: centering life in the insatiable demands of the ego is the sure path to doom. . . . They know that life confined to the self is a prison, a joy-killing, neurosis-producing, disease-fermenting prison."[4]

The challenge in giving self a proper place is to avoid incurring double damage. On the one hand, allowing the urges of self to flow unchecked will lead to the inevitable damage that selfishness inflicts on its victims. On the other hand, denying the human need to understand and value oneself will lead to personal insecurity, emotional emptiness and relational poverty.

NURTURING A MATURE "SPINE OF IDENTITY"

Nurturing a mature self includes developing a strong spine of identity. A spine of identity becomes a part of you; it is simply inherent in your presence. When you engage in conversations with moral consequences or face complicated situations that require careful decisions, you draw on its innate strength. For there to be such strength, however, you must intentionally nurture the inner life of the mind, the conscience and the soul.

The absence of a spine of identity and clear self-concept would leave us morally wobbly, emotionally vulnerable and subject to interpersonal exploitation. Our need is to give proper attention to the formation of self without becoming excessively self-focused. We must deliberately deal with the making of *me*.

A strong spine of identity clarifies our self-definition and positions us to live with coherence. We can stand on the solid ground of chosen values and defensible ethics. We live within a framework from which to respond to life's expectations and demands. We can approach unknown situations believing we have the capacity to draw from an informed behavioral repertoire. Our established boundaries give us the confidence to stand apart from the accepted cultural norms without feeling rejected. The reflective insights of our furnished mind sensitize us to the complexities and ambiguities of our world. The convictions of our conscience empower us to keep wresting with what is right and good. And the beliefs that are rooted in the substance of our soul energize us to keep working out our faithfulness to our loving God.[5]

I do not want to point to some panacea that would simplify life and remove all feelings of anxiety. But clarifying our self-definition does address the enemy with a smiling face of "character without design." Consolidating our self-concept positions us to link the *being* of our designed character with the *doing* of our behavior. The lifelong process of maturing our spine of identity allows us to access our best self most of the time.

ACCEPT WHAT YOU CANNOT ALTER

The word *demography* comes from the Greek word *demos,* meaning "the people." When sociologists attempt to explain "the people," they often divide personal demographic characteristics into two categories. The first category, *ascribed* characteristics, includes all personal identifiers over which people have no control, such as age, ethnicity, race and sex. The second, *achieved* characteristics, includes identifiers over which we have at least some control, such as income, occupation and education.[6]

Whether we like it or not, we all are endowed with a particular gene set over which we have no say. The color of our skin, the age of our body, our height, the color of our eyes, our basic temperament and the range of our intelligence are all part of our human permanence.

As much as we may dislike some of these characteristics, they are the essence of our uniqueness. Rather than agonizing over what we cannot alter, we are better served by addressing what we can affect. Healthy self care includes accepting what we cannot change.

ALTER WHAT YOU CAN CONTROL

What sociologists call our "achieved characteristics" is where we are challenged to alter what needs to be altered. We all know people who live like dimming 75-watt light bulbs. They have the basic skills to survive and pursue modest achievements. But along life's journey they encountered struggles that overwhelmed them; their confidence waned so that now, without being socially disruptive, they limp through their days and nights. Their stories contain more sadness than joy. They keep lowering their expectations without being noticed very much by people around them.

There is another group of people who live like 250-watt light bulbs that will always get brighter. They are gifted. Their personality attracts others to them. They make the dean's list without studying very much, play the dating game with flair, excel at sports if they want to and decide which job to take from a list of offers. People who are 250-watts are physically appealing, socially poised, and as far as anyone can tell, personally secure. However, they have at least one fatal flaw. They can coast on their inherent abilities and neglect the disciplined hard work it takes to develop their potential. In their early years, these gifted coasters achieve their goals readily. In the long run of life, though, they become mediocre. Their bright light of promise fades. The only reason they deserve to be pitied is that they could have achieved much more. They could have excelled in their vocation, contributed to society and offered exceptional gifts to the people who share their world.

Laws of life are inescapable. Whether the power of our personal wattage is 75 or 250 or somewhere in between, if we do not pay the price of altering what we can control, we will be controlled by what we do not alter. Healthy self care calls us to pay the price.

RECONCILE YOUR ROLES

There is another challenge to address on the road to becoming what God desires us to be. It involves reconciling our various life roles by integrating what we believe into each sphere of our existence. The task is difficult. Integration is the highest level of behavior to reach for and achieve. And our limitations leave us with inevitable inadequacies.

Often I feel like a player in an identity scramble. My multiple roles press me to juggle the distance between my lofty ideals and my flawed reality. I'd like to get all the roles right, but they frequently overwhelm me:

- family member
- father
- spouse
- grandfather
- employee
- supervisor
- proud Canadian
- neighbor
- author and public speaker
- advocate for the poor
- committed follower of Jesus

I believe my Christian faith makes it possible to experience an integrat-

ing identity, an identity that can be coherently expressed in all the roles
life asks me to play. I move in that direction by asking, *What is my dominant identity? What is the major focus I can rely on to integrate my attitudes
and behaviors?*

My response is decisive. I want to be a faithful follower of Jesus
Christ. I know I won't get it right all of the time, but I also know what
my spiritual aspirations call me to become. Whether I am relating to my
wife and grandchildren, enjoying banter with my Jewish neighbors, engaging people at the office or in a cultural situation different from my
own, I want to be *Don, follower of Jesus.* I sense that the God of creation,
the Holy Spirit who both affirms and convicts, wants that too.

CELEBRATE YOUR "I AM" SCRIPT

John the Baptist knew who he was and who he was not. When interro-
gated by his critics, he was ready to declare, "I am not the Christ, Elijah
or the prophet. I am not worthy to fasten the sandals of the One who is
yet to come." His disclaimer was part of his identity.

John the Baptist was also ready to make statements of self-affirmation:
"I am the voice" of someone who is still to come. "Look" at someone who
is greater. Consider "the Lamb of God who takes away the sin of the
world" (see Jn 1:15-28). John emptied his backpack of "I am nots" so he
could fill it with "I ams."

Christian mystic Simone Weil clarifies a related dimension of self-understanding: "It is a fault to wish to be understood before we have made ourselves clear to ourselves."[7] Not only did John the Baptist have a clear grasp
of himself; his greatest self-insight was that he defined himself in reference
to Jesus. He affirmed his uniqueness in relationship with the greatest person who ever walked on planet earth. He rooted his identity in Christ's in-
comparable stature. And in doing so, he was able to affirm his chosen self.

Jesus was also clear about his identity. He readily declared his "I am"
script. "I am the vine. I am the good shepherd. I am the door. I am the
way, the truth and the life." Although his spirit agonized in the Garden
of Gethsemane, it was his deep-rooted confidence that "I and my Father
are one" that marched him to the cross.

Clearly Jesus was a one-time, never-to-be-equaled person. His "I am" statements can only be his. Still, his presence in history is meant to be a model and to lift the level of our lives. Within our human limits, our "I am" declarations can be definitive. Rooted in our emerging self-definition, we can assert and celebrate our "I am" script. With God's help, I am and will be

- trustworthy
- teachable
- forgiving
- a loyal friend
- a responsible employee
- an empathic boss
- a faithful spouse
- an unrelenting follower of Jesus
- an unfinished work of art

DIRECTION FOR THE JOURNEY

To be fully alive is to exist in a state of constant becoming. We may retire from our vocation and attend the funerals of our friends and spouse, but our aspiration to mature our spine of identify should not end. Discerning self care can continue until we enter into eternity with a "well done" welcome.

In the meantime, Robert Wuthnow wisely counsels, "faced with growing uncertainties and with ample opportunities for choice, people will need to spend more time than ever before reflecting on the deep values that make life worth living and the sources of those values, including spirituality."[8]

As we sort through the opportunities, make our choices and work out our salvation, we pray, "Grant that we may seek not so much to outwit as to outlove" those with little or no regard for God's good ways.

16 Soul Care

Scripting My Story in God's Story

People today are spiritually thirsty. Whether they have a churched or some other background, people are yearning and open to experiencing a "taste and see" spirituality. This searching is not specifically Christian in its scope. The desire to be touched by something transcendent is expressed in encounters with angels and with crystals, in ESP and communication with the dead, in searches for nirvana and encounters with Jesus. The quest can produce a nonrational mix-and-match spiritual collage.

Recently I was in a taxi with a driver whose headgear signaled that he was a Muslim. Yet a decorative cross dangled on a leather thong from his rear-view mirror. Intrigued, I asked, "I'm interested in the cross that is hanging from your mirror. Are you making a personal statement?"

"I'm a Muslim, but I have respect for the cross," he responded. We continued discussing our different views of Jesus until we reached my destination. My taxi driver showed me that mix-and-match spirituality is not limited to people with a Christian background. In these times of growing interest in religion and the transcendent, fragmented spirituality is present among other faiths as well.

"Before Christians get too excited about the renewed interest in religion," writes Mike Riddell, "it is well to note that the emerging culture's exploration of spirituality is in many ways a reaction against institutional Christianity as it has been experienced in the West."[1] As a result today's spiritual questing is more individual than institutional, more personal than socially concerned. The everything-and-anything embrace of divine experiences has little to do with the demands of traditional religion which seek to alter one's character and change one's conduct. Eugene Kennedy of Loyola University in Chicago speaks of a "soft spirituality. Enjoying spiritual feelings without spiritual ideas . . . a spirituality that is more about shadow than substance."[2]

The "Miss Manners" columnist observes that a growing trend is people's informally and spontaneously creating makeshift shrines, often connected to a public tragedy, such as the death of Princess Diana.[3] The cultural mood of the moment nurtures the replacement of conventional religion with indiscriminate expressions of spirituality.

Today we should expect people to seek spiritual satisfaction in secular ways. Social researcher Michael Adams, speaking with a thirsty soul, contends, "I believe, beyond doubt, that we can live quite happily in a secular world. But that is not to say a life without meaning."[4] Don't be surprised when musicians in concert halls and bars open their sets with comments like "Here is a gospel song for secular people; you know, all the spirituality without the inconvenience of Jesus."

GOD'S VULNERABILITY

The movie *Notting Hill* did not win any Academy Awards, but it did include some images and dialogue that merit attention. Hugh Grant portrays William Tucker, an ordinary guy, the proprietor of a small travel bookstore. He is an underachiever, a member of a profoundly strange family. Cast as a famous movie star named Anna Scott, Julia Roberts plays a role closer to her own life.

Anna and William have various low-key encounters that begin in the bookstore. Attracted to each other, they exchange a kiss here and there, and eventually there is a little discreet sex. Their relationship is tentative, intriguing and almost intimate, but more imaginary than real. Then another man in Anna's life pushes William to the sidelines. The film communicates the deep pain they both feel.

After months of separation, William and Anna reunite. The high-profile, sought-after movie star appears before the ordinary guy and declares with transparency and tenderness, "I'm here to see if you could like me again."

William responds, "My fear is I'll just be cast aside again."

Then with contrite vulnerability Anna pleads, "The thing is . . . I'm just a girl, standing in front of a boy . . . asking you—will you love me? Hoping you will love me . . ."

In another script, one that is profoundly *un*predictable, the Creator and Redeemer of the universe stands before people everywhere, reaching out with striking vulnerability, "I'm just God, standing in front of you . . . asking you—will you love me?

"I'm just Jesus, standing in front of you. My invitation is straightforward. Come to me. Come with your histories, your good and bad intentions, your beauty and your brokenness . . . come with your sin. I'm here in your presence hoping we can learn to love each other."

GETTING IN TOUCH WITH GOD

The matter of *how* we come to Jesus has been inseparably woven into church history. For centuries, all around the world, people were expected to come to the church to stand before God and receive forgiveness and light. Today the majority of the world's Christian family continues to hear the invitation to come to the church and receive the sacraments as a way of coming to Jesus. Come to the waters of baptism to be marked with God's presence and welcomed into the Christian family. Come repeatedly to the Eucharist in remembrance of Christ's death and resurrection and be enlivened to worship and serve.

During the past century and particularly in the last fifty years, the evangelical way of coming to Jesus has gained in prominence and redemptive effectiveness. Articulated by the anointed voice of Billy Graham and other evangelists, the call to personal conversion has marked a turning point in church history. The evangelical way of coming is more precise and more prescribed than experiencing God's forgiveness through the church and the sacraments. The biblical call to "repent of your sins and believe on the Lord Jesus Christ" in order to be saved implies there is a specific time when one's conversion happens. The "hour of decision" in a particular time and place becomes the spiritual watershed.

Youth specialist Gerard Kelly contends, "If there is any one aspect of Christian practice that is roundly challenged by postmodernity, it is a turnstile understanding of conversion—the view that a single decision, made in a moment, is enough to secure lifelong commitment."[5] The Scriptures show people coming to faith in different ways. One example is Paul on the road to Damascus (Acts 9); another is two disciples walking with Jesus on the Road to Emmaus (Lk 24). One reinforces conversion as a decisive event. The other images people on a journey eventually becoming aware of Jesus and accepting God's will and ways.

Jesus' encounter with Paul is a dramatic affair. Paul's moment of conversion radically changed him from a persecutor of the faith into a proclaimer of Jesus as the true Son of God. Paul's fervor, the energy that went into opposing Jesus and his ways, was remarkably transformed into a divine vision that lifted up Jesus and led to the establishment of the New Testament church.

The story on the Road to Emmaus is quieter. Following a hectic day in Jerusalem, two men are taking a seven-mile journey mostly minding their own business when Jesus joins them. Although they have heard the news and rumors that Jesus was crucified and his body has disappeared, they do not recognize that it is Jesus who is now walking with them. Jesus, realizing the two are well informed but do not understand the significance of what God is doing around them, expresses some frustration. Then he turns to his teacher mode and offers a history lesson explaining what it all means. The two men's eyes are still blind to Jesus, and they don't get what he is attempting to teach them. It is only when they are eating together and Jesus takes bread and breaks it that they recognize who he is.

A short account of my faith journey would combine dimensions of the dynamic experience of conversion with divine interventions along the way. Moses experienced a series of divine interventions during his life. His encounter of an intervening God in the burning bush (Ex 3) resonates with me.

In my spiritual history, there have been moments when God's Spirit has touched my spirit in special ways. I remember a childhood encounter with God that left me feeling both energized and forgiven. In my struggle with doubt, a series of events helped me make the transition from *believing in* God to *knowing that* God exists. At times the Holy Spirit has confronted me for patterns of behavior that were heading in destructive directions. Recently in worship, I was preparing to receive the Lord's Supper and, with good intent, was virtuously offering myself to God. But God intervened. In my consciousness Jesus communicated with me: "You've got the order wrong—I have already given myself to you. Relax!" It was a treasured and holy moment in a holy place.

During a Sunday worship service in Washington, D.C., before the time for passing the peace, the priest said, "It would be a shame to leave here without knowing those around you." Then he paused and said slowly, "It would be a much greater shame to leave here without knowing God." This statement was followed by extended applause, as if people were telling God, who was in their presence, that they had no intention of leaving without knowing him.[6]

The good news is, we can know God in personal and powerful ways. God's personal nature invites a personal response. And God reveals more and more to us along our journey. God is not a static noun but a dynamic verb. Simply debating about how people come to faith or restricting faith to knowledge about God would be like trying to understand a train by studying the station timetables. We have to take the journey to experience it.

Reducing God's ways of working with people down to a particular method or church ritual is really an attempt to bring the almighty God under restrictive human control. The issue is not *how* we get in touch with God but *if* we get connected with God.

STAYING IN TOUCH WITH GOD

In the past it was assumed that staying in touch with God meant it was necessary to be actively involved in a church. Author and speaker Marva

Dawn helps us see how those of us who attend public worship are now viewed by those who choose not to attend: "To worship the Lord is—in the world's eyes—a waste of time. It is indeed a royal waste of time, but a waste nonetheless. By engaging in it, we don't accomplish anything useful in our society's terms."[7]

Let's face it, churches are divine-human creations that can be excessively human. We go to church expecting to receive spiritual help, and sometimes we end up getting spiritually damaged. No wonder many people move around from church to church and others choose to remove themselves from church life for periods of time.

Idealized and romantic views of church life will certainly end up being discarded in the land of disillusionment. However, trying to live as a Christian without actively participating in a church community is a long-term strategy for spiritual apathy and departure from the faith. Although it is relatively easy to gather church naysayers and encourage them to articulate their pain and disdain, the church is God's idea. The challenge of Christian believers is to partner with God in nurturing the Church to fulfill its ordained purposes. One of those purposes is to keep people in touch with Jesus Christ, who "loved the church and gave himself up for her" (Eph 5:25).

Christian churches and religious traditions are like people. In order to claim an identity, they have to be different from each other. People have distinctive markings: temperament, personality, appearance, convictions, behavioral patterns. Churches have distinctive markings: beliefs, governance, rituals, worship style, lifestyle expectations. The intriguing question to ponder is: What is my personal spiritual style, and is my church's primary spiritual style compatible with my preferred spiritual style?

Just as there are different ways and methods to get in touch with God, there are different spiritual styles that help us stay in touch with God. In a world that makes incessant demands on our time, increasing numbers of people are finding meaning in expressions of *contemplative spirituality*. Worship that includes reflection and times of silent prayer feeds the soul of people who experience the presence of God in quiet meditation. In

contrast, people who are drawn to a *charismatic spiritual style* are energized by more dramatic, life-empowering encounters with the Holy
Spirit. Whether it is worshiping with hands lifted high or privately
speaking in tongues, charismatic Christians celebrate the Spirit's presence in their life with exclamation points. *Evangelical spirituality* may or
may not include expressions of the contemplative or the charismatic, but
it is marked by biblical preaching that speaks to issues and clarifies doctrine with a clear, authoritative voice. Those who worship in evangelical
churches are also expected to witness to their personal reality of Christ's
salvation to people they encounter. Those who are oriented to *sacramental spirituality* affirm the sacredness of their life in Christ with ceremonial
worship. The sacraments, in particular the Eucharist, symbolize and express their faith in God's will and ways. Within these and other expressions of Christian spirituality, different churches will give different em-
phases to social justice issues: what it means to live a holy life and what's
involved in pursuing Christ's mission in our world.[8]

Although individual churches within a denomination or Christian
tradition may vary from the norm, churches with particular labels gravitate to particular spiritual styles. For example, Baptists, as splintered
and diverse as they are, still distinguish themselves as evangelicals. Pen-
tecostals can be counted on to be charismatic. Nazarenes and Wesleyans
urge holiness of life. Catholics and Anglicans center on sacramental beliefs and practices. Historic Protestants and Catholics are the churches
most likely to put emphasis on social justice concerns. And churches
that are sacramental are more likely to be contemplative than those that
are charismatic in their worship style.

For a positive church experience, it helps to be part of a faith community that envisions the Christian life and celebrates worship in ways that
are in harmony with one's personal spiritual style. Even if one's family
was in a particular denomination, or if one came to first-time faith
through the influence of a certain church, one's personal spiritual style
may or may not mesh with that church style. People's long-term spiritual
development is best served when there is compatibility between their
personal spiritual style and that of the church they attend.

Clarifying and nurturing our spiritual style also helps us understand and deal with some of the enemies with smiling faces. If our personal commitment includes both the evangelical and social justice spiritual styles but we attend a church where *either* personal faith *or* social action is the only message we hear, the dissonance will generate increased discomfort. When the worship and preaching tone rings with spiritual superiority that offends our desire to express both conviction and compassion, our continued participation in that church can be damaging to our spiritual health. If we increasingly become committed to live as Christian Collaborators but are participating in a Tribalizer church, we will know we do not belong. For the sake of unity in the kingdom, and for the sake of our spiritual survival, it will be better to switch than fight.

When we find ourselves in a church where our personal spiritual style is in conflict with the organizational style, we wonder whether we should stay and seek to be an influence for what we believe is the better way or choose to move on. The challenge is to avoid taking action that damages the community *or* staying in the situation too long and being damaged for doing so. Whatever the scenario, we will be better able to discern God's direction if we commit more time to prayer than we spend talking about the problems on the phone.

Unfortunately, our good intentions to stay in touch with God can be hindered and uprooted by many different forces. However, we cannot blame our church experience for our spiritual failures. In the end we have to take responsibility for our own spiritual well-being. As Thomas Merton says, "The spiritual life is first of all a life. It is not merely something to know and be studied; it is to be lived. Like all life, it grows sick and dies when it is uprooted. . . . If we want to be spiritual, then, let us first of all live our lives."[9] In other words, going to church alone is not a magic potion to guarantee our spiritual health. How we implement the theory of faith into our daily living will either grant us spiritual coherence or produce patterns of spiritual dissonance.

Our practices of reflection, prayer and service when we are away from church and no one is watching will either put substance in our faith or sentence us to shallowness. We will keep spiritually rooted only as we

continually return to stand before Jesus in both our beauty and our brokenness. We will keep connected when we are close enough to hear
God's Spirit whisper, "I'm here in your presence, hoping we can keep
learning to love each other."

DIRECTION FOR THE JOURNEY

The changes and challenges of life in our world tend to make us pull
back from the unknown and huddle in the comfort of the known. Anyway, we scurry around frantically just to keep up with the routine.
Rather than making room for more of God's revelation, we pull the
blinds down on what might be next. Our lack of understanding of and
appreciation for spiritual styles different from our own keep us from being enriched by what has meaning for others. When life is thus reduced
to reruns, we miss the possibility of discovering and living the mysteries.

Radio alarms wake us up. The news is a breakfast companion. Car
CDs soothe us. Elevator music serenades us. Office telephones control
us. E-mail barrages us, and cell phone conversations turn us into eaves-
droppers. We need to slow down the pace, turn down the noise. We
need to escape the cultural clatter. If we turn down the noise, we will
have a chance to tune in to what we need to hear.

We need space to listen to our inner voice and the voice of the Holy
Spirit. Cultivating the art of reflection will protect us from drowning in
noise. It will slow us down so we can nurture the guidance systems that
reside in all of us. And when we are quiet, we will hear when God
speaks. "Silence, the contemplative knows, is that place just before the
voice of God."[10]

After we have heard the voice of God, we will be able to get on with
writing the sacred script that will be best for us and the people who share
our lives—seeking not so much to outwit people as to outlove them.

17 Outreach

Making Meaning of God's Gospel Story

If the social analysts, cultural critics and postmodern pundits are right, influencing people with little interest in the Christian faith to seriously consider getting in touch with God will be a challenging venture in these times. We are told that stories like creation and the cross are viewed with suspicion as grand narratives and meta-stories too grandiose to be plausible, let alone believable. Relativism reigns, truth is a matter of personal opinion, and it is impossible to know anything for sure. The cultural consensus celebrates multimindedness and outlaws one-way mindsets. Although searching for a particular version of spirituality is considered virtuous, claiming that there is a single source of truth is tantamount to judging others, and that is socially and morally unacceptable. Surely we are mature enough, the line of logic goes, to accept that objectivity is unattainable and subjectivity is inevitable. Evangelists who invade the space of others and seek to impose their views break the rules of the spirit of the age. "Respect my right to be me," is the retort. "Tune in to the times: preference is principle, so my preference is my valid principle."

Those of us who have been trained to expect God's Spirit to work only within the constraints of particular methods will likely be unsettled by these times. The spirit of the age may appear to be more potent than the past norms that conditioned many of our expectations. Others of us simply feel intimidated by what we sense is happening.

One way of dealing with these puzzling times is to envision God as an artist—an artist of the nontechnique. Instead of restraining God to predictable patterns, we will realize that the action of the Spirit is like the wind: we don't know where it comes from or where it goes (Jn 3:8). It is also helpful to image ourselves as couriers of a multidimensional gospel. Just as courier companies deliver items in different-sized packages to different customers, God wants us to communicate with different people in different ways—ways that make meaning for them in their particular circumstances.

GOD AS ARTIST

God is an artist of the nontechnique. When it comes to inviting people to believe and follow Jesus Christ, the process is a divine drama. Repeating standardized methods is simply not God's way of attracting and welcoming new people into the Christian family.

The experience of a Chinese student who immigrated to Canada from Hong Kong illustrates God's highly personal way of working. In the new English-speaking college setting, people found his Chinese name extremely difficult to pronounce. His solution was to change his name to Simon. Why Simon? He liked the music of Simon and Garfunkel (and I suspect he concluded that taking the name Garfunkel would not help him much).

On campus, Simon met another student who remarked that his name was like that of one of Jesus' disciples. Simon explained why he had changed his name and acknowledged that he knew nothing about Jesus or the names of his disciples.

As the two became friends, the Canadian did the natural thing and asked, "Why don't you come to our church with me?" Simon readily accepted the invitation, and in the months that followed, he became a Christian and started living as a disciple of Jesus.

God's ways of working became clearer for me during a spiritual storytelling segment in a service at my church. David told us, "As a South African living in the midst of entrenched apartheid, it was when I saw a white church welcome blacks into their congregation that I first thought, *Jesus must really make a difference.* I didn't understand it all at the time, and I still don't, but that's when I started the journey I am on."

Gerard Kelly reinforces the divine pattern with his insight into the encounter between Jesus and Nicodemus. "Jesus issued a direct challenge to this wise old man so scared of change that he crept to the appointment under cover of darkness. He called him to swap his competence for newness; his knowledge for ignorance; his certainties for mysteries; his faith in a static, unchanging God for a living relationship with the wind that 'blows where it pleases.'"[1]

In East Africa people often use the expression "Leave it to God!" Rather than being fatalistic, I suspect the saying developed out of a genuine trust in God in the midst of painful circumstances. Jesus' engagement with Nicodemus and the stories of Simon's and David's coming to faith make me smile and exclaim, "Leave it to God! Leave it to God to do something like that—something so highly personal and improbable." Just as your divine drama is exclusively yours and my story is uniquely mine, we can expect God to script the stories of others with continuing creativity.

PARTNERS IN DIVINE DRAMAS

Though God's ways are immensely creative, it is still important for people who want to help communicate God's good news to function within a biblical framework. Unless there is some plot in the script, there will be random chaos instead of drama. Scholars Anthony Pappas and Scott Planting look out at all of creation and define Christian mission as "participating with God in the transformation of human life—individual, corporate, and institutional."[2] On a more individual level, Christian mission can be understood as inviting people to encounter the gospel story, to let the story of creation and the cross enter into their personal story so that their story is radically altered. They renounce some dimensions of their past and replace them with a new script.

Obviously there are numerous ways to think about mission and making meaning for people. One helpful approach is to envision the expressions of mission and soul care outreach within the framework of *a theology of place* and *a theology of people*.

A theology of place frames Christian mission in a specific geographical location. Churches represent best the central idea of a theology of place. They exist as faith communities within a broader community. The residential presence of churches positions them to engage, serve, offer programs and welcome the people in the surrounding community. Churches that take their theology of place seriously remain flexible enough to change their ministry focus when the demographics of the neighborhood shift around them. If their setting is urban, they resist being lured to the suburbs.

A theology of people invites a mindset that motivates ministry wherever God's people go. Rather than being residential, a theology of people assumes that ministry is mobile and itinerant. Such ministry celebrates people's spiritual gifts and counts on interpersonal interaction and the flow of influence in relationships. Mission impact is dependent on the spiritual integrity and the social skills of those who intentionally live outreach lifestyles. The ministry influence is not dependent on someone's simply having a flair for words, however. A theology of people mindset cherishes the presence of Christ that is resident in people of faith and counts on that presence within relationships and interactions. Gabriel Moran reminds us that "teaching by example means first and mainly living with people and showing, by the way one lives, a way of life. . . . The way people learn goodness or virtue is by the presence of good, virtuous people."[3]

Methods and language. No matter what we decide to do, we cannot escape decisions about methodology. Whether the task is as mundane as vacuuming the carpets or as challenging as witnessing creatively, we have to make choices about how to do what we want to do. Well-intentioned, often passionate people have produced a plethora of evangelistic tools in recent decades. Some would contend that these printed booklets and designed scripts inviting people to come to Christ are part of God's orchestrated divine drama. Others see them as legitimate and sometimes effective, but they prefer other ways of making the claims of Christ known. No matter how we assess the effectiveness of various methods of reaching out, we should avoid becoming captive to any single method.

Language too can imprison us if we do not remain alert. Like people in every other vocation and profession, Christians develop distinctive language sets and code words. Within some Christian groups, using magic mantras is the way to confirm your orthodoxy. Punctuating sentences with "Praise the Lord" and "Thanks be to God" can make you an insider with those who use those expressions but an outsider with those who don't. When one claims to be "born again" or "saved" in the presence of fellow Christians who talk in a similar way, there is commonality. But those same words are mystifying and sometimes offensive to other faithful followers of Christ. And outside the Christian family, however, the code words are confusing. Instead of making meaning for people, such "Christianese" is a foreign language.

Walter Brueggemann issues the right challenge: "In the modern world, Christians need to be bilingual." They need to "speak the language of both the religious tradition and the 'empire' with whom members must deal."[4]

Questions and dialogue. Recently I was having breakfast at a hotel in Zambia where the tables were crammed together. The two European gentlemen seated very near me were obviously well-known frequent guests. They were having a conversation with the restaurant manager that I could not ignore.

Christians in Zambia are often open about their faith and freely speak of it in public. The restaurant manager, a person of great social poise and vivacity, was one of those people. Unable to resist, she spoke of how important her faith in God was to her. "I have a sense of inner peace. I know that God is in charge of what is happening around me."

The European men responded readily. One of them declared, "When you die, you go straight to the grave. That's all there is to life."

The manager was a little shocked, but she was not defensive: "I could never believe that. Jesus has promised us heaven."

Later the second man volunteered, "I'm a Christian, but I'm not religious."

The woman would not accept such confusion and replied, "Well, I'm a religious Christian, and you should be too."

In human terms, the restaurant manager gave the Holy Spirit a lot to work with. But I wanted to jump into the conversation with questions. "How did you come to the conclusion that the grave is all there is? I'd like to understand more about how you are constructing your life."

Then, "I'm intrigued by your statement that you are a Christian but not religious. I've never heard anyone say that before. What do you mean?"

Questions engage people and prompt them to reflect. They turn monologues into dialogues and transform mini-sermons into personal stories. Questions also linger. Until they are resolved, they can leave people pondering.

Admittedly, questions can be manipulative and controlling. We have no right to ask questions if we are not genuinely interested in the answers. Posing clever questions is not a game to play. But if we care about people and want to engage them in meaningful dialogue, asking sincere questions opens doors.

"What's your religious background?" is a question I ask frequently, because almost everybody has one; a religious identity is a part of who people are. In my experience it is rare for people to shy away from talking about theirs. And often after telling me about their religious history, people will pointedly ask, "What is *your* religious background?" The exchanges are mutually enriching. How God's Spirit works in the midst of the exchange is up to the artistry of God.

THE GOSPEL, A MULTIDIMENSIONAL STORY

"Christianity is very firmly perceived as part of the old order," John Drane notes, "and therefore something to be discarded rather than trusted for the future."[5] Because people do not automatically link their spiritual interest with what the Christian church offers and because many think they've heard it all before, we need to reconfigure our conventional ways of Christian truth-telling. Certainly the gospel story will always be God's changeless story, but the need today is to tell the old news in new ways.

How can we become spiritual meaning-makers for the people God brings within reach of our personal contact and potential influence? How can we creatively and faithfully participate in the divine dramas being played out in the lives of people around us?

There are common connecting points that cross cultures and climb up and down socioeconomic ladders. Sensitively explored, life themes allow us to reveal God's hope for creation and Christ's role in redemption. Engaging people in conversations around themes such as purpose and meaning, relationships, values, ethics and choices can lead to life-changing encounters.

Purpose and meaning. The aftermath of the September 11 terrorist attacks was devastating for the airline industry. My route to the office goes directly by the airport, and within a few days after it was announced that a charter airline had been placed in bankruptcy, eighteen jet aircraft appeared on the tarmac. Weeks went by and they never moved. With the tips of their wings almost touching each other they stayed parked side by side adjacent to a busy runway. I kept thinking, *What a tragedy. What a waste. Eighteen planes perfectly able to fly. And they just sit there.*

Some people's lives are like that. They are born to fly, but for myriad reasons they are grounded. They have all the equipment they need to fulfill God's purpose for them, but they are parked on the side of life's runway.

There is good news for grounded people. God has designed everyone to fly. The God who created people with purpose in mind eagerly wants to help parked people accelerate down the runway. God wants us all to believe that people who are parked on the tarmac can get off the ground. Faith is believing that God makes it possible for people to find their wings.

Relationships. People ache to be loved. Life without human relationships is stark and empty. Life without a relationship with God leaves us incomplete and vulnerable to our own will and ways. We are created for so much more.

God's self-disclosure as Father, Son and Holy Spirit reveals the relational nature of the God who loves and desires relationships with all people. Restoring our broken relationship with God positions us to build strong relationships with the people who share our life.

Values and ethics. All values do not have equal virtue. Generosity shines in the presence of greed. All ethics are not equally moral. Honesty rings with rightness while cheating and lying come at someone else's expense.

Christians who take their faith seriously are called to develop value and ethical guidance systems. As God's people we don't get it all right all the time, but we are equipped to live positively with others and to go to sleep with a clean conscience.

Existing without a set of coherent values and ethics in these "my preference is my principle" times turns people's daily lives into moral scrambles. There is good news to share. God's intervention transforms disarray into design and randomness into coherence.

Choices. An affluent society that encourages and entices people to pursue their personal preferences creates a complex culture. And dealing with complexity demands making lots of choices. It is no wonder that we feel overchoiced and underinformed.

Discerning God's preferential choices does not turn us into robots, but it does give us a multidirectional compass for finding our way. Life in Christ positions us to make right choices, positive choices, for the sake of ourselves and for others.

The gospel is multidimensional. It relates to the breadth of our lives. Figuring out what God has to do with life's issues brings clarity to our own lives. Engaging others in this process gives them opportunities to respond to their situations in ways that include God. And when the major issues of life are in order, enemies with smiling faces can be kept in check.

GOSPEL THEMES

Last week Rudy told his spiritual story. He didn't come from what he called a "churched family." Neither did he have a circle of Christian friends in his history. He did, however, come from what he called a "solid family." His parents loved each other and were "responsible members of the community." In Rudy's terms, his education was complete, and his career was on track, but there was something missing. "My mind was unsettled. My spirit was restless."

At this point in the story we see God the Artist at work again. "I'm not even sure where it came from, but in my library there was a Bible that someone had given me. It was one of those modern versions, just the New Testament. I began reading it, and I kept reading and thinking. Don't ask me to explain all that happened, but after about six months I'd read most of that Bible a couple times and I just believed it. It became clear. One night I said Jesus was for me."

Without interaction with others, Rudy learned the gospel story from the Holy Spirit and the Scriptures, and God became part of Rudy's story. The content and meaning of the gospel made sense, settled Rudy's mind and redirected his life. The Bible's *gospel themes* focus us on the core of God's revelation. They are gifts from God to pass on to others. Gospel themes reveal what the God of creation and the Christ of redemption still dream about and hope for. They are the theological content of our faith. When we communicate the gospel's themes to others in ways that are understandable and applicable to their lives, they can build their faith with biblical content too.

God's truth, biblically revealed and personally experienced, continues to be the foundation for our faith. In times past, proclaiming God's truth was often all that was needed to prompt people to believe the truth. As Os Guinness shows, today's truth picture is different:

> There is no truth: only truths. There is no grand reason: only reasons. There is no privileged civilization (or culture, belief, norms and style): only a multiplicity of cultures, beliefs, norms and styles. There is no universal justice: only interests and the competition of interest. There is no grand narrative of human progress; only countless stories of where people and their cultures are now.[6]

How can any of us have confidence in our own version of truth?

In the current cultural milieu, the Christian challenge is neither to give up believing God's truth nor to flaunt God's truth as a trump card that ends conversations. Effective faith sharing will be more concerned about leading people to discover truth than starting with predetermined truth announcements and "the Bible says" declarations.

God's baseline for human redemption is Christ's death on the cross and resurrection from the grave. The uniqueness of Christ rests here. The credibility of all the claims of Christian faith stands or falls here. Our hope to get in touch with God and stay in touch with God resides here. Without the cross and resurrection there is no salvation and no coming of the kingdom. The central message of the cross is reconciliation—between us and the God of creation, between one human being and another, one community and another. The message of reconciliation rings true in the midst of widespread conflict and brokenness in our world.

Reconciliation and forgiveness are our gifts through Christ's cross. The good news to share is that God's invitation into a divine-human relationship restores and transforms people's lives.

Righteousness and justice are social consequences of the cross in our broken world. God's command to love, to do what is right and to seek justice, is meant to restore societies and transform cultures.

The story to tell is that in a remarkable and unpredictable way, God intervened and sent Jesus to make salvation possible, to mediate our protection and to energize our obedience. Making meaning for people around the gospel themes of truth, the cross and resurrection, reconciliation and righteousness can nurture faith that has substance and strength.

REASONS FOR HOPE

Though communism is in demise and the Cold War is in the past, instead of being able to take sighs of relief, we now face the trauma of terrorism and new revelations of despicable corporate corruption. Every day the media deliver graphic reasons for gloom and doom. Sometimes we feel as if we're being buried in an avalanche of bad news. The issues are so massive and complex that we can easily feel helpless and conclude that even if we care we cannot make any difference.

Still, many people are looking for reasons for hope and practical direction. They want to know how to make life work. An effective outreach strategy for making sense out of the Christian faith is seeking to articulate Christian views on current issues.

Biblical scholar Richard Longenecker asserts, "By observing how the New Testament writers used the early Christian confessions in addressing the various issues, circumstances, and mind-sets of their day, we can gain insight into how the gospel was contextualized in the first century and receive direction for contextualizing this same gospel today."[7] The following list of issues seems daunting, but these topics do open opportunities to engage in conversations that invite people to consider and respond to distinctive Christian views.

- corporate corruption
- lust for money
- abuses of political power
- justification of war
- euthanasia and abortion
- human rights and children's rights
- racism and inequality
- perpetual poverty
- gender inequities
- sexuality issues
- new family structures
- relating to world religions

The complexity of the issues takes away any temptation to oversimplify the journey to Christian clarity and coherence. Even though wrestling with complex issues is hard work, surely the alternative is not to lapse into bitter complaining about the dreadful state of the world. It is only when we take time to think and discuss messy issues that we are able to not only develop views that are distinctively Christian but also paint positive pictures of how God wants us to live together.

METAPHOR AND STORY

As I sat across the lunch table from Peter, I could sense his pain. His children were going in directions that alarmed him and his wife. His church was caught up in disruptive conflict. His work environment was increasingly unstable. Faced with such pressures, Peter's spirit was in turmoil.

My question to him was direct: "How is your faith helping you deal with your pain?"

Without a moment's hesitation he responded, "Right now my life is like a spider's web. I have a few anchor points. There aren't very many, but my experience of God's presence in the past is enough to give me confidence that I can withstand the problems in the present." For the moment, "anchor points" was the metaphor that was keeping Peter's life intact.

Missiologist David Bosch aptly states that "metaphor, symbol, ritual, sign and myth, long maligned by those interested only in 'exact' expressions of rationality, are today being rehabilitated. . . . They not only touch the mind and its conceptions, and evoke action with a purpose, but compel the heart."[8]

Creating metaphors and other visual messages can help us communicate God's truth. For example, the presence of television is pervasive in most parts of the world. Increasingly, access to cable and satellite dishes is producing exposure to scrambled TV channels. If we choose not to subscribe to cable services, we must channel-surf our way through static sound and distorted images. Is it possible that life without God is like watching a scrambled cable TV channel? Images fill the screen, but we can catch only occasional glimpses of the story being portrayed. Unable to appreciate the art form that the writers, actors and directors imagined, we are left feeling incomplete and dissatisfied. The metaphor suggests the question, why not subscribe to the Creator's will and ways and get the complete story in brilliant color with static-free sound?

In our age of the omnipresent computer, we can image God as software for our human hardware. After all, God the Creator was the original programmer. Only God knows what it takes to "have life, and have it abundantly" (Jn 10:10). Our great temptation is to load our self-designed software, which will inevitably distance us from life in Christ. God's custom-designed software is stored and ready to be loaded into our human spirits. Revelation in Scripture is software for our mind. God's compassion protects us from human viruses. The presence of the Holy Spirit gives us energy to both resist what destroys life and pursue what enables life.

Creating new metaphors should not replace our reliance on the Scriptures, but they can be meaning-makers for particular people. Metaphors are also invitations to our imagination to explore new paths of communication that can reenergize our desire to share the gospel with freshness.

Leonard Sweet makes a case for spiritual storytelling: "Jesus' life was not an essay. Jesus' life was not a doctrine. Jesus' life was not a sermon. Jesus' life was a story. People don't live essays or doctrines or sermons. They live stories. People are not pulled from the edge of the pit by essays or doctrines or sermons. They are rescued by stories. They are healed by stories."[9]

Not only was Jesus' life on earth an astonishing story; he was also a remarkable storyteller. When Jesus told the parable of the prodigal son, he knew his listeners could identify with the characters. The party-animal younger brother, the stay-at-home "I'm better than you are" elder brother and the filled-with-pain father continue to be points of identity for audiences everywhere.

Stories are more powerful than lectures or strung-together points of propositional truth. Rather than pointing accusing fingers or sending signals of judgment, stories create space for people. Stories invite people into a drama. Without threatening people, stories compel their listeners to compare their story with what they are seeing and hearing. They create room for the Spirit of God to linger. It is no wonder that stories get remembered and repeated.

In a culture in which individuals are valued over institutions, there is power in sharing personal stories. When grand narratives like the creation and redemption story claim too much certainty and are just too big for many people to believe, the claims of personal experience are indisputable. Telling about events in one's life can invite people to try out God for themselves. God's story embedded in our stories plants seeds of the possibility that others can experience God too.

One temptation, of course, is to downsize the grand gospel narrative to the size of our personal stories. Rather than stifling our spiritual storytelling, however, the danger should serve to remind us that God's grace is the source of our continuing story.

DIRECTION FOR THE JOURNEY

As followers of Jesus, we live with convictions. We believe the gospel is true. We believe that God's will and ways revealed in the life, death and resurrection of Jesus are meant for all peoples.

Frederick Buechner reminds us that "in the last analysis, you cannot pontificate but only point." A Christian is one who points at Christ and says, "I can't prove a thing, but there's something about his eyes and his voice. There's something about the way he carries his head, his hands, the way he carries his cross—the way he carries me."[10]

Touched by God and believing that others can also be touched, we keep finding our way—sometimes listening, sometimes speaking, sometimes asking questions, sometimes answering inquiries, sometimes making an overt appeal, seeking not so much to outwit people as to outlove them—and intrigue them.

18 Social Care

Pursuing God's Justice Story

In the beginning when God put the finishing touches on creation, the Garden of Eden was a paradise. Its beauty and absolute serenity would have overwhelmed a *National Geographic* photographer. There was no threat of smog or acid rain. People were present in the garden, but there was no selfishness, no unresolved anger or hate, no deceit, no violence or shame, no injustice of any kind. God was present in the garden. And because there was no life-denying presence, God was content there.

God's ideal of paradise in the Garden of Eden is long gone from planet earth. Although there are many moments when beauty startles us, and there are seasons of serenity, life is wracked with pain that turn dreams into nightmares. Repeatedly, potential paradises tumble into brokenness.

God's historical pattern of response to the brokenness and nightmares has been to intervene. Noah was an intervention. Moses, Abraham, Joseph, Elijah and Esther were all God's interventions. Jeremiah, Isaiah, Micah, Amos and Hosea were people who tuned in to God's aspirations in their times and gladly became instruments of divine intervention.

Jesus did more than make a casual visit to our planet. His Father in heaven did not send him to us with only a tourist visa in his pocket. In the fullness of time, Jesus came with a work permit and a job description to fulfill. Christ's surrender on the cross became God's ultimate intervention. Jesus' life, death and resurrection still stand as God's triumphal act in history to end the nightmares and rescript broken dreams.

Although Jesus finished the work he came to achieve, as followers of Jesus we too have a job description to fulfill and a mission to complete. We are to work together in Christ to bring hope and reconciliation into our present battered and unjust world. In our times, the people of God remain in the brokenness of the world as instruments of divine intervention.

Those of us who aspire to follow Jesus and his ways are meant to be a redemptive presence: to affirm God's original desires for creation, to walk with people in their nightmares and to point the way to renewal and restoration. This mandate for the church is much broader than expressing concern for individuals who are spiritually indifferent and confused. The call is to intervene in the name of Christ when communities and cities are places of pain and abuse, when people are denied their right to human dignity, and when the faithful are persecuted and injustice reigns. Lest we forget: "Civilization is not a gift, it is an achievement—a fragile achievement that needs constantly to be shored up and defended from besiegers inside and out."[1]

GOOD SAMARITAN BEHAVIORS

Some of God's saints who celebrate their personal faith in Christ are not so ready to embrace the gospel as service and justice for others. Robert Logan and Larry Short articulate a continuing tension: "On one side are those fervently committed to the task of world evangelism and wanting to see heaven populated with redeemed individuals. On the other side are those whose hearts break for hurting humanity where oozing emotional and physical sores are graphic reminders of the flawed condition of the human soul." But Jesus never struggled with such compartmentalization. "Demonstrating compassion and simultaneously seeking the conversion of the heart were irrevocably welded and intertwined in the mind and ministry of the Son of God."[2]

Jesus sets the standard for responding to hurting humanity with the story of the good Samaritan (Lk 10:29-37). He also reveals the cost of getting involved with others. "Moved with pity," the Scriptures say, the Samaritan surrenders his schedule to the needs of the man bleeding in the ditch. He also takes money out of his wallet and lays down his credit card to cover future expenses.

Time and money are the cherished currencies of modern culture. The paradox is that very often those who have time on their hands have very little money and those who can write generous checks live with too little time. Jesus does not detail the personal circumstances of the Samaritan, but he does call us to good Samaritan behaviors. The cost of caring is paid in the two currencies of our world: time and money.

The Power of Deeds

A sign painted on the window of a bankrupt bookstore tells another cultural story: "Words Failed Us!" Words alone have lost much of their power. Too many voices have broken too many promises for us to trust either the messengers or the words they proclaim. The sheer volume of information that washes over us in a twenty-four-hour period makes it impossible to weigh what is important or monitor what may or may not be verifiable.

Speaking with a prophetic voice decades ago, Francis Schaeffer underscored the importance of *doing* the truth: "Unless people see in our churches not only the preaching of the truth but the practice of truth, the practice of love and the practices of beauty, . . . they will not listen, and they should not listen."[3]

A friend who lives on the island of Newfoundland tells me that her father grew up as a committed Protestant Christian, convinced like so many around him that Catholics could not be Christians. Catholics simply believed too many things that conflicted with his Protestant convictions. In his latter years, my friend's father had a serious heart attack that severely limited his physical activity. He and his wife were forced to move from their rugged rural setting into the city. In God's good providence, their new next-door neighbors were Catholics.

One morning after the move my friend was talking to her father on the phone. "You know that our next-door neighbors are Catholics," he said. "They sure are faithful in their church attendance. But the bigger point is, they have really looked after your mother and me. They take us shopping every week and are very careful to carry our groceries right into the kitchen. When it snows, they clear our driveway before they look after their own." After a thoughtful silence, the father stated his conclusion: "I think our Catholic neighbors must be Christians." The language of deeds speaks with persuasive power.

We learn to be virtuous the way we learn to speak a language. Just as some people speak their language better than others, some people's lives are more virtuous than others. We need to learn from those who live virtuous lives. In the coming years in our society, demonstrating godly virtues will be more influential than eloquent godly talk.

COMMUNITY ACTION

Seeking to correct what has gone wrong in society usually requires collective action: marshaling resources and mobilizing groups of people. Rather than resting on individual initiatives, our concern to correct injustice will more likely be expressed within our church and orchestrated through organizations. Challenging churches to act, Brazil's Bishop Robinson Cavalcanti exclaims, "We cannot wait for the devil to die a natural death. Our mandate is to interfere with history. Our permanent call is to fight against the darkness and to fight for the needs of people."[4] The unfinished Christian mission includes plunging into the world's mess even when we know the mission will not be completed in our lifetime. As Jacques Ellul states, we get involved "not in the hope of making [earth] a paradise, but simply in order to make it more tolerable."[5]

There is a midsized city on the West Coast that has more than its share of large churches. On Sundays you have to think about traffic patterns and finding a place to park if you want to be on time for the call to worship. The churches' exemption from property taxes became an issue of injustice in the mind of one of the city's elected counselors, who put forward a motion that the churches be required to produce evidence that they deserved their favored tax status. His criterion was reasonable and straightforward: "Produce tangible evidence that your social contribution to the community equals the taxation benefits your churches receive."

The city's ministerial had to schedule some extra late-night meetings to respond to this challenge. In the end they were able to retain their favored status, but the city counselor's challenge also led to a new cooperative social-service ministry.

If your church or my church burned down on Sunday night, would anyone in the community who doesn't attend our church be adversely affected in the next six days? What value do churches bring to the communities surrounding them? If they were to disappear, who would care?

Community-concerned and justice-committed churches matter to the people who live in the surrounding neighborhood. Although families may not attend, they are aware that the church is a community contributor. Few complain about the extra parked cars on the streets on Sundays. They don't complain because they remember being impressed when they were contacted during the church's community needs assessment. They know that money raised from basement sales goes toward supporting young single parents. They have received invitations to "Parenting Teens" and "Dealing with the Damage of Divorce" seminars. They remember that it was people from the church who rallied the neighborhood against changes to zoning laws that would have permitted a porn shop to take up residence. They know that at considerable expense "those church people" have sponsored a refugee family and donated furniture to set up the new apartment. The neighbors know about the senior shut-ins who receive regular visits and nourishing meals. They have watched the church youth group spend a few hours doing a spring cleanup at the house across the street where death had made an untimely visit a few weeks earlier. And they wish they could have supplied the drinks for the pizza party that followed. In neighborhoods where there are community-concerned churches, residents think privately, *If we ever decided to go to church, the church around the corner is the one we would attend.*

Community-action churches are serving churches. Martin Luther King Jr. says it beautifully: "Everybody can be great because everybody can serve. You don't have to have a college degree to serve. You don't have to know about Plato and Aristotle to serve. You don't have to know Einstein's theory of relativity to serve. You only need a heart of grace. A soul generated by love."

CONTRIBUTING TO CIVIL SOCIETY

"When the church does what it is supposed to do," asserts Dorothy Bloom, "it transforms not only the lives of its members, but the life of their culture as well." In so doing we affirm "the biblical concerns for freedom, equality, community and justice."[6] When those concerns are present in our communities, they become important building blocks of our civil society.

The value and importance of a civil society doesn't make the 6:00 news or the front page of the newspaper. In North America we assume that our shared life in society basically works. Consequently, we don't always make the connection between being a good citizen and preserving a just society. Our inclinations are more directed toward being good parents and responsible employers and employees than toward being guardians of our social order.

On the church front, seminary professor Craig van Gelder suggests, "people no longer assume that the church has anything relevant to say on matters beyond personal faith. Public policy became increasingly secularized, as public morals became increasingly privatized."[7] On the business front, Anita Roddick contends that companies have become "hypnotized by the bottom line and forgotten their moral obligations to civil society. The prevailing view of trade could be described as commerce without a conscience." Roddick personally asserts, "I'd rather promote human rights than a bubble bath."[8]

Beyond having access to justice in the courts, freedom of the press and the right to free speech, a good society as envisioned by Don Eberly is a "society with shared values and personal and social order. It consists of positive ideals, strong communities, civility, and manners. It can neither be doled out as just another entitlement, nor pieced together through programs, nor stimulated into existence by tax cuts. Instead it must be achieved through the cooperative efforts of individuals from all sectors of society."[9]

A good society will be constituted by citizens who are ready to seek the common good for everyone. A civil society must come to terms with the inherent diversity within any population living in shared cultural and geographical space. If there is to be political order rather than social chaos, civility is the deliberate duty of all citizens.

Fuller Seminary president Richard J. Mouw interjects an important qualifier: "Being civil doesn't mean that we cannot criticize what goes on around us. Civility doesn't require us to approve of what other people believe and do. It is one thing to insist that other people have the right to express their basic convictions; it is another thing to say that they are right in doing so."[10] Constructive dissent, then, is not just a democratic right; it is a sign of intellectual and moral discernment as well as a quality of civility.

Along with our prayers and constructive dissent, what should today's Christians contribute to civil society? Certainly it would be possible to create a short list in response to the question. I propose that our Christian gift to today's civil society is *an unrelenting concern for justice.* If followers of Jesus do not speak out and act on behalf of those who are marginalized and voiceless, who in modern society can be counted on to do so? As Nicholas Wolterstorff points out, "When the Bible talks about justice and injustice, it doesn't start giving us a litany of the perpetrators. It gives us a litany of the victims, the wounded ones—the widows, the orphans, the aliens."[11]

God's mandate to pursue justice is not about preserving my almighty rights and privileges. Rather, biblical justice is about

- standing alongside social outsiders
- amplifying the voices of the marginalized
- challenging indifference toward the vulnerability of the poor
- opening doors of opportunity for the powerless
- protecting those who are thought to be the weak
- transforming impersonal stereotypes into human faces with names

- addressing systemic conditions that keep destroying hope
- advocating fairness and chances to begin again
- being instruments of intervention on behalf of the victimized

Justice in God's order of creation is celebrating the reign of righteousness with those for whom life has gone wrong.

EFFECTIVE CHURCHES

Influencing public policy and bringing social transformation require collective action. Effective churches can choose to serve as collective instruments of justice and social change. In order to do so, however, they develop definitive ministry models to inform their strategies.

Clergy and lay leaders of these kinds of churches are able to sketch the ministry model of their church on a napkin over coffee in a restaurant. And when you visit their church and examine what really happens in the programs and among the people, life isn't perfect, but the theory translates into practice.

I recently encountered one of these churches, First Assembly in Calgary, Alberta. As I had supper with members of the council committee and a few of the pastoral staff, they explained their ministry model with great clarity.

The four words on their napkin are *Personal, Social, Local* and *Global*. First Assembly people have (1) passion for their personal faith, (2) compassion for people with social needs, (3) sensitivity to their local context and (4) empathy for long-distance global poverty. In their words: "We exist to make Christ's last command our first priority. . . . Ultimately, we desire to minister the whole gospel to the whole person using the whole church."

When you walk into the church, it feels warm but also worn. A large map of the world is prominently posted. After a fast-paced tour, I asked the senior pastor, "Why all this emphasis on caring for the world?"

He slowed down for a moment and said, "Every night when I was growing up, my mother prayed us around the world."

First Assembly is blessed with energetic and visionary leadership. But its vision does not belong to just the pastor. According to one of the council members, "The priesthood of believers is not theory for us. We believe that every Christian has gifts, skills and talents. People's lives preach the message." All fourteen people around the table that night had led mission teams made up of people from their church. Their approach is straightforward: "Instead of a wallet-sending church, we are a people-sending church. We are not just givers. We are senders."

Personal. The source of the people's energy and vision is no secret. They are motivated by their personal faith—their enabling and sustaining life in Christ.

Social. The vitality of their personal faith is what generates social concern. "The approach is to help people catch the vision of caring for the poor, the widow and the orphan as a response to God's Word—not just a heartfelt reaction to human need."

Local. Decision-makers at the church are presently finalizing legal arrangements to convert a seven-story hotel into a "Dream Centre" to serve the needs of street people. In the words of one of the mission council members, "The church serves as a means to mobilize people; it does not serve itself."

Global. The church's Global Training Institute equips its people for short-term missions. On the first weekend of every month, the focus is on global missions. The format does not involve pastoral voices exhorting people to go into all the world. Members of the church who have been on mission trips tell their stories and share their vision. Collectively, the church has had a ten-year commitment to respond to the HIV/AIDS pandemic in Uganda and sub-Saharan Africa. Linked with a church in Uganda, it has purchased numerous pieces of property where orphans receive special care and a sense of Christ's love for them.

I suspect there is a certain amount of disarray in this church. There is too much vision, too many ideas and too much to get done for life to be orderly. I'm told there aren't as many expensive cars in the church parking lot as there used to be. But when you think about it, what is the gospel and what is the church? Could it be about keeping first things first and "existing to make Christ's last command our first priority"?

DIRECTION FOR THE JOURNEY

My piano-playing career ended early. Although I officially passed level six, my technique was more a matter of memory and rote than the expression of an artist. One symbol on the musical score that I do remember enjoying, however, was the accent. Whenever I saw that mark, I knew I had permission to pound out that bar of the piece with all the muscle I could muster. The result would not have pleased the composer, but the added crescendo did make me feel better.

Jesus' challenge to the scribes and Pharisees is about getting the accent right, adding volume in our life so that the Creator God is able to say, "We've got it right." Listen to Jesus' concern: "Woe to you, scribes and Pharisees, hypocrites! For you tithe . . . and have neglected the weightier matters of the law: justice and mercy and faith. It is these you ought to have practiced without neglecting the others" (Mt 23:23). In other words, scribes and Pharisees, you've got the accent wrong. Among the other important matters of faith, you need to emphasize justice.

Jesus' encounter with the Pharisees tends to trouble me. I feel hypocritical myself. Although I'm a strong believer in the centrality of justice in the Christian life, when I'm honest, the longing to be loved and the desire to love are often more powerful in me than a yearning for others to be given justice.

Without escaping my dilemma, I do wonder whether, systemically, being loved and having the capacity to love are what really generate a persevering accent on justice. Perhaps it is only when we receive God's love with all the enabling power God's Spirit generates in us that we will find ourselves really yearning for justice for others.

How then can we get the accent right? When love and mercy and forgiveness flow from God to us, we are touched and changed. God's loving presence in us becomes the fuel for justice. We are energized to speak perceptive words and do strategic deeds. We are motivated to bow down and discern what to groan in our prayers. We are guided to pursue personal and organizational advocacy, to defend people exploited by those with unchecked power, to champion the dignity of children and to create opportunities for people who have inherited unbearable circumstances. We dream and lobby, we provoke and pursue, we envision and push for progress that transforms a less humane world into a more humane world.

Maybe all those piano lessons weren't a waste after all.

Maybe, with the energizing presence of God's Spirit, our spirit will be transformed so that we seek not so much to outwit people as to outlove them.

Epilogue

In today's puzzling world, we are vulnerable if we remain naive. Idealism is simply too ideal to work. Bowing to "what works," though, entails too high of a moral risk. Opting for rugged individualism puts too much pressure on any human being. Simply selling out to an all-embracing social consensus lacks the integrity of personal discernment. So what can we do?

In the public forum, irony becomes a posture to protect against taking anything too seriously. Clever humor sends the message that nothing is too sacred to be mocked. Cynical skepticism is preferred to anything that sounds like certainty. Late-night TV hosts wield sarcasm to probe others' views with ridicule. Editorial commentators pour passion into their computers, shoot their bullets and then hedge their bets. These cultural shapers state their views, sell their wares and keep their jobs while avoiding the accusation of believing too much or the dreaded vulnerability of appearing to be naive.

Enemies with smiling faces feed on naive people. Over time they devour followers of Jesus who surrender themselves to unexamined beliefs housed in self-contained organizational and doctrinal systems. They crush Christians who conclude they are spiritually superior to other followers of Jesus. The smiling-face enemies also seduce people who stake their lives on the worldly assumption that life without God is life as it is meant to be. They leave self-constructed people—whether "ordinary" or "gifted"—scrambling to fulfill their self-envisioned destiny.

In the public forum and in circles of personal relationships, the Scriptures offer ways to resist being captured by the enemies. "Watch out for deceptive voices, worldly voices making promises, Christian voices calling for commitments that don't fit into Christ's will and ways. Beware of enemies with smiling faces" (Col 2:8, my paraphrase). Beware of misleading voices. Beware of Christian voices that distort Christ's ways while claiming to have exclusive access to God's views and values. Beware of worldly voices that make promises too grandiose to be kept, that trumpet self-sufficiency and the right to self-define life's agenda.

The Scriptures do more than simply send out warnings. They invite positive action: "Since you have received Christ Jesus, live like it. Go deep and build up your faith, expressing a thankful spirit" (Col 2:6-7, my paraphrase). The biblical invitation is to celebrate our life in Christ and build up our faith. Minimalist beliefs are not enough. The cry of the heart is to experience the God of grace and mercy. Still, the complexities of the day require faith that has substance and frameworks that can help us make our way through difficult ambiguities. One of the continuing challenges of living with integrity in these times will be to live with a thankful spirit—to give more than we take. One secret for dealing effectively with the complications of day-to-day life is to be more concerned about doing good than about rebuking evil.

When the Eucharist is being served in our church, we sometimes sing a Taizé chant, the words of the thief who was crucified next to our Lord:

Jesus, remember me, when you come into your kingdom.
Jesus, remember me, when you come into your kingdom.

In the end, living without naiveté and counting on Jesus to remember you and me will be enough.

Notes

Chapter 1: Quick-Fix Faith

[1]Gerard Kelly, *Retrofuture: Rediscovering Our Roots, Recharting Our Routes* (Downers Grove, Ill.: InterVarsity Press, 1999), p. 67.

[2]Lesslie Newbigin, *Truth to Tell: The Gospel as Public Truth* (Grand Rapids, Mich.: Eerdmans, 1991), p. 32.

[3]Dallas Willard, *The Spirit of the Disciplines* (San Francisco: Harper, 1988), p. 15.

[4]Elton Trueblood, *The Predicament of Modern Man* (New York: Harper & Brothers, 1944), pp. 59-60.

[5]George H. Gallup Jr. and Timothy Jones, *The Saints Among Us* (Harrisburg, Penn.: Morehouse, 1992), p. 20.

[6]William Spohn, "Practice Rather than Preach," *Theology Today* 33, no. 9 (2000): 5.

[7]Stanley Hauerwas, *Unleashing the Scripture: Freeing the Bible from Captivity to America* (Nashville, Tenn.: Abingdon, 1993), p. 9.

[8]Flannery O'Connor, *The Habit of Being: Letters* (New York: Farrar, Straus & Giroux, 1979), p. 478.

[9]Dietrich Bonhoeffer, *Life Together* (San Francisco: Harper & Brothers, 1954), p. 40.

Chapter 2: Feeling-Only Faith

[1]Françoise Champion, "15-20 ans: croyez-vous en Dieu?" (Fifteen-Twenty-Year-Olds: Do You Believe in God?), *Phosphore,* December 1994, p. 8.

[2]Blaise Pascal, quoted by Robert Coles, *The Secular Mind* (Princeton, N.J.: Princeton University Press, 1999), p. 125.

[3]Kim Howland, "Seeker Churches," *Christian Century*, March 7, 2001, p. 24.

[4]Sven Birkerts, interview by Katherine Kellogg and Stuart Hancock, in *Mars Hill Review*, no. 15 (Fall 1999): 75.

[5]Michael Horban, "On Going Beyond What Is Written," *Resource: The National Leadership Magazine,* November-December 1966, p. 4.

[6]Norman Lamm, quoted by Rahel MusLeah, "Religions Update—The Road Soon Taken," *Publishers Weekly* 246, no. 46 (1999): S8.

[7]Howland, "Seeker Churches," p. 24.

[8]Robinson Cavalcanti, paraphrased from my notes during a speech in Brazil, December 1999.

[9]Paul Wilke, *The Good Enough Catholic: A Guide for the Perplexed* (New York: Ballantine, 1996), p. 8.

[10]Eugene Kennedy, *The New World*, August 30-September 6, 1998.

[11]Catherine Hare's account of her experience is published as *A Hope and a Future: A Young Widow's Journey Through Grief* (London: Hodder & Stoughton, 1996).

[12]Stanley Crouch, *Books & Culture*, May/June 1998, p. 3.

Chapter 3: One-Sided Faith

[1]Ronald J. Sider, *One-Sided Christianity? Uniting the Church to Heal a Lost and Broken World* (Grand Rapids, Mich.: Zondervan, 1993), p. 25.

[2]David O. Moberg, *The Great Reversal: Evangelism Versus Social Concern* (New York: J. B. Lippincott, 1972), p. 23.

[3]The BBC TV program, whose title I do not have, aired April 15, 2000, in Geneva, Switzerland.

[4]Mark Noll, *The Scandal of the Evangelical Mind* (Grand Rapids, Mich.: Eerdmans, 1994), p. 141.

[5]William H. Willimon, *The Intrusive Word: Preaching to the Unbaptized* (Grand Rapids, Mich.: Eerdmans, 1994), p. 39.

[6]Bob Pierce, quoted in Graeme S. Irvine, *Best Things in the Worst Times: An Insider's View of World Vision* (Wilsonville, Ore.: BookPartners, 1996), p. 17.

[7]Carl S. Dudley, *Basic Steps Toward Community Ministry* (New York: Alban Institute, 1992), p. xii.

[8]John Drane, "Was God in Dunblane?" *Baptist Times*, March 21, 1996, p. 8.

[9]Henry T. Blackaby and Claude V. King, *Experiencing God* (Fort Worth, Tex.: Broadman & Holman, 1994), p. 138.

[10]Quoted in Dudley, *Basic Steps Toward Community Ministry*, p. 52.

[11]Sider, *One-Sided Christianity?* p. 117.

[12]Vernon C. Grounds, *Evangelicalism and Social Responsibility*, Focal Pamphlet 16 (Scottsdale, Penn.: Herald, 1969), p. 23.

[13]Richard J. Mouw, *Uncommon Decency: Christian Civility in an Uncivil World* (Downers Grove, Ill.: InterVarsity Press, 1992), p. 168.

Chapter 4: Spiritual Superiority

[1]Stephen L. Carter, *The Culture of Disbelief* (New York: BasicBooks, 1993), p. 25.

[2]Edmund Morgan, ed., *Puritan Political Ideas: 1558-1794* (Indianapolis: Bobbs-Merrill, 1965), p. xiii.

[3]S. D. Gaede, *When Tolerance Is No Virtue* (Downers Grove, Ill.: InterVarsity Press, 1993), p. 62.

[4]Larry Christenson, *A Charismatic Approach to Social Action* (Minneapolis: Bethany Fellowship, 1974), p. 17.

[5]Brian McLaren, "Honey, I Woke Up in a Different Universe," *Mars Hill Review*, no. 15, Fall 1999, p. 41.

[6]Vernon C. Grounds, *Evangelicalism and Social Responsibility*, Focal Pamphlet 16 (Scottsdale, Penn.: Herald, 1969), p. x.

[7]Neil Postman, quoted in Theodore J. Wardlaw, *Journal for Preachers*, Lent 2000 <ctsnet.edu/newsandpublications/JournalforPreachers/mainpage.htm>.

[8]John Hick, *Truth and Dialogue* (London: Sheldon, 1974), 148.

[9]Paul Wilke, *The Good Enough Catholic: A Guide for the Perplexed* (New York: Ballantine, 1996), p. xiv.

[10]Kelly Brown-Douglass, "Taken Out of Context," *Context*, August 15, 1997, p. 8, quoting *The Other Side*, March/April 1997.

[11]Tom Harpur, "Every One of Us Walks with a Limp," *The Toronto Star*, January 12, 1997.

Chapter 5: Depreciating the Image of God

[1]Samuel H. Miller, *The Dilemma of Modern Belief* (New York: Harper & Row, 1963), p. 108.

[2]Jean Vanier, interview, "Living with People with Disabilities," *Envision*, Spring 2001, p. 11.

[3]Susan Newhook, "Am I a Person Born in the Image of God?" *Globe and Mail*, August 6, 2001, p. R7.

[4]Eugene Rivers, "The Responsibility of Evangelical Intellectuals in the Age of White Supremacy," in *The Gospel in Black and White: Theological Resources for Racial Reconciliation*, ed. Dennis L. Okholm (Downers Grove, Ill.: InterVarsity Press, 1998), p. 17.

[5]Ibid., p. 16.

[6]James Q. Wilson, *The Moral Sense* (New York: Free Press, 1993), p. xii.

[7]Ibid., p. 55.

[8]Ibid., pp. 99-101.

Chapter 6: Self-Construction

[1]Jean Bethke Elshtain, "The Gift Economy," *Tikkun* 15, no. 1 (2000) <www.findarticles.com>.

[2]Lesslie Newbigin, *Foolishness to the Greeks* (Grand Rapids, Mich.: Eerdmans, 1986).

[3]Mike Regele, *Death of the Church* (Grand Rapids, Mich.: Zondervan, 1995), p. 80.

[4]Phillip E. Johnson, "Nihilism and the End of Law," *First Things*, March 1993, p. 20.

[5]Reginald Bibby, *Mosaic Madness* (Toronto: Stoddart, 1990), p. 98.

[6]Robert Coles, *The Secular Mind* (Princeton, N.J.: Princeton University Press, 1999), p. 11.

[7]Anne Lamott, *Traveling Mercies: Some Thoughts on Faith* (New York: Pantheon, 1999), p. 100.

[8]C. S. Lewis, *The Great Divorce* (London: Geoffrey Bles, 1946), pp. 66-67.

Chapter 7: Affluenza

[1]Neil Postman, *The End of Education: Redefining the Value of School* (New York: Alfred A. Knopf, 1995), p. 33.

[2]David Hilfiker, quoted in Martin Marty, "In God We Trust—Not Anymore," *Context*, October 1, 1998, p. 3.

[3]Michael Kearl, "Quotations," *Seeds*, quoted in *Living Pulpit*, April/June 1998, p. 32.

[4]John Wesley, "Evangelicalism: Faith-Sharing or Market Share?" *Wheaton Alumni*, Summer 1999, p. 5, quoted in Nathan Hatch, *Context* 31, no. 22 (1999).

[5]Douglas Coupland, *Polaroids from the Dead* (London: Flamingo, 1997), p. 161.

[6]Ron Sider, "The Ethical Challenges of Global Capitalism," *Discernment*, Winter 2001.

[7]G. K. Chesterton, quoted in Leland Ryken, *Redeeming the Time: Approaches to Work and Leisure* (Grand Rapids, Mich.: Baker, 1995), p. 67.

Chapter 8: Character Without Design

[1]Lesslie Newbigin, *The Gospel in a Pluralistic Society* (Grand Rapids, Mich.: Eerdmans, 1989), p. 1.

[2]Gary Dorrien, *Soul in Society: The Making and Renewal of Social Christianity* (Minneapolis: Fortress, 1995), p. 339.

[3]Wendy Murray Zoba, *Generation 2K* (Downers Grove, Ill.: InterVarsity Press, 1999), p. 98.

[4]Thomas L. Friedman, *The Lexus and the Olive Tree* (New York: Anchor, 2000), p. 31.

[5]Robert Wuthnow, *After Heaven: Spirituality in America Since the 1950s* (Berkeley: University of California Press, 1998), p. 165.

[6]Larry L. Rasmussen, *Moral Fragments and Moral Community* (Minneapolis: Fortress, 1993), p. 12.

[7]Rick Reilly, "A Paragon Rising Above the Madness," *Sports Illustrated,* March 20, 2000, p. 136.

[8]I. Howard Marshall, "Towards Maturity," quoted in Rowland Croucher, ed., *Still Waters Deep Waters* (Oxford: Albatross/Lion, 1987), <www.pastornet.net.au/jmm/articles/11345.htm>.

[9]James Garbarino, quoted in editorial, *The Independent* (London), April 30, 1999.

[10]Cornelius Plantinga Jr., *Not the Way It's Supposed to Be: A Breviary of Sin* (Grand Rapids, Mich.: Eerdmans, 1995), p. 21.

[11]Lawrence Cunningham, "Glad You Asked: Q & A on Church Teaching—What is the 'Dark Night of the Soul,' " *U.S. Catholic,* January 2001, p. 33.

[12]Martin Luther, quoted by J. I. Packer, *Freedom, Authority and Scripture* (Leicester, U.K.: InterVarsity Press, 1981), p. 31.

Chapter 9: Privatized Faith

[1]The percentage is higher in Canada than in the United States.

[2]Stephen King, *On Writing* (New York: Simon & Schuster, 2000), p. 61.

[3]The main categories are Catholic, Protestant (mainline, evangelical, Pentecostal, independent) and Orthodox.

[4]Peter L. Berger, *The Desecularization of the World: Resurgent Religion and World Politics* (Grand Rapids, Mich.: Eerdmans, 1999), p. 15.

[5]Wendy Doniger, "Religion and Science Unite," *Radcliffe Quarterly,* p. 1, quoted in *Context* 32, no. 11.

[6]Robert Griffin, former C.S.C. chaplain at Notre Dame, quoted in Luis Gamez, "Death Where Is Thy Tweak?" *Notre Dame Magazine,* Winter 1999-2000, p. 6 <www.nd.edu/~ndmag/griffw99.htm>.

[7]Rodney Stark and Charles Y. Glock, *American Piety: The Nature of Religious Commitment* (Berkeley: University of California Press, 1968), pp. 15-16.

[8]Karl Rahner, *The Religious Life Today* (New York: Seabury, 1975), p. 8.

[9]Hervé Carrier, *Evangelizing the Culture of Modernity* (Maryknoll, N.Y.: Orbis, 1993), p. 138.

[10]Robert Wuthnow, *Christianity in the Twenty-first Century* (New York: Oxford University Press, 1993), pp. 5-6.

[11]Carrier, *Evangelizing the Culture,* p. 138.

[12]Alice Camille, "Long Live the King," *U.S. Catholic* 65, no. 11 (2000): 50.

[13]Richard J. Foster, *Prayer: Finding the Heart's True Home* (San Francisco: HarperSanFrancisco, 1992), p. 1.

Chapter 10: Dealing with Diversity

[1]Angela Ellis-Jones, *Times Literary Supplement,* December 27, 1996, p. 8.

[2]Ovide Mercredi and Mary Ellen Turpel, *In The Rapids: Navigating the Future of First Nations* (Toronto: Penguin, 1993), p. 2.

[3]S. D. Gaede, *When Tolerance Is No Virtue* (Downers Grove, Ill.: InterVarsity Press, 1993), p. 63.

[4]Rick Warren, *The Purpose Driven Church* (Grand Rapids, Mich.: Zondervan, 1995), p. 156.

[5]Don E. Eberly, *Restoring the Good Society* (Grand Rapids, Mich.: Baker, 1994), p. 84.

[6]Hans Küng, *Global Responsibility: In Search of a New World Ethic* (New York: Crossroad, 1991), p. 55.

[7]George Carey, during a visit to Egypt and Sudan, *The Anglican Journal,* March 2001, p. 8.

[8]Douglas John Hall, *The Future of the Church: Where Are We Headed?* (Toronto: United Church Publishing House, 1989), p. 57.

[9]Paul Marshall, "True Pluralism Is Grounded in God's Patience," *Christian Week,* April 27, 1993, p. 3.

[10]Miroslav Volf, *Exclusion and Embrace: A Theological Exploration of Identity, Otherness and Reconciliation* (Nashville: Abingdon, 1999), p. 29.

[11]Martin E. Marty, "Conclusion: Proselytism in a Pluralistic World," in *Pushing the Faith: Proselytism and Civility in a Pluralistic World,* ed. Martin E. Marty and Frederick E. Greenspahn (New York: Crossroad, 1988), p. 158.

[12]Volf, *Exclusion and Embrace,* p. 101.

[13]John Gray, "Where There Is No Common Power," *Harper's,* December 2001, p. 15.

Chapter 11: Balancing Conviction and Compassion

[1]This conviction-compassion typology was first developed and published in Donald C. Posterski, *True to You: Living Our Faith in Our Multi-minded World* (Winfield, B.C., Canada: Wood Lake, 1995).

[2]Patrick Glynn, *Brookings Review,* Spring 1999.

[3]Richard J. Mouw, *Uncommon Decency: Christian Civility in an Uncivil World* (Downers Grove, Ill.: InterVarsity Press, 1992), p. 21.

[4]Frederick Buechner, *Telling Secrets* (San Francisco: Harper, 1992), pp. 63-64.

[5]James Fowler, *Weaving the New Creation* (San Francisco: Harper, 1991), p. 151.

[6]Richard F. Lovelace, *Dynamics of Spiritual Life* (Downers Grove, Ill.: InterVarsity Press, 1979), pp. 16-17.

[7]John Paul II, *Crossing the Threshold of Hope* (Toronto: Alfred A. Knopf, 1994), pp. 80-81.

[8]Naomi Wolf and Frederica Matthewes-Green, "Finding Common Ground," *Sojourners* 28, no.1 (1999): 32-35.

Chapter 12: Dignifying Cultural Differences

[1]Dan Doolittle, quoted by Don Posterski and Gary Nelson, *Future Faith Churches: Reconnecting*

with the Power of the Gospel for the Twenty-first Century (Winfield, B.C., Canada: Wood Lake, 1997), p. 152.

[2]Neil Bissoondath, *Selling Illusions: The Cult of Multiculturalism in Canada* (Toronto: Penguin, 1994), p. 177.

[3]Peter L. Berger, *A Far Glory: The Quest for Faith in an Age of Credulity* (New York: Doubleday, 1992), p. 67.

[4]Miriam Adeney, quoted in Chris Wright, "Christ and the Mosaic of Pluralisms," in *Global Missiology for the Twenty-first Century: The Iguassu Dialogue,* ed. William D. Taylor (Grand Rapids, Mich.: Baker Academic, 2000), pp. 74-75.

[5]Miroslav Volf, *Exclusion and Embrace: A Theological Exploration of Identity, Otherness and Reconciliation* (Nashville: Abingdon, 1999), pp. 53-54.

[6]Stephen Kliewer, *How to Live with Diversity in the Local Church* (New York: Alban Institute, 1987), p. 12.

[7]Michael Ignatieff, *Blood and Belonging: Journeys into the New Nationalism* (Toronto: Penguin, 1993), p. 6.

[8]Ibid., p. 37.

[9]Craig Van Gelder, *The Essence of the Church* (Grand Rapids, Mich.: Baker, 2000), p. 109.

[10]Dallas Willard, "No Pluralism in Moral Matters?" *Discernment* (Wheaton College), Winter 1994, p. 2.

[11]Jung Young Lee, *Marginality: The Key to Multicultural Theology* (Minneapolis: Fortress, 1995), p. 10.

[12]Justice Kenneth MacKenzie, British Columbia Court of Appeal, quoted in Rod Micklebourgh, *The Globe & Mail,* September 27, 2000, p. A3.

[13]Alan Dershowitz, quoted in Martin E. Marty, "A Skeptic: I Don't Believe It," *Context,* November 15, 1999, p. 3.

[14]S. D. Gaede, *When Tolerance Is No Virtue* (Downers Grove, Ill.: InterVarsity Press, 1993), pp. 37-38.

Chapter 13: Global Citizenship

[1]Thomas L. Friedman, *The Lexus and the Olive Tree* (New York: Anchor, 2000), pp. 6-7.

[2]John Kenneth Galbraith, *The New Industrial State,* 2nd ed. (Boston: Houghton Mifflin, 1971), pp. 208-9.

[3]Joseph Epstein, "Show Me the Money," *Times Literary Supplement,* July 23, 1999, p. 4.

[4]Ron Sider, "The Ethical Challenges of Global Capitalism," *Discernment,* Winter 2001, p. 2.

[5]R. C. Longworth, "A Grotesque Gap," *Chicago Tribune,* July 12, 1999, p. 1.

[6]Michael Novak, "The Ethical Challenges of Global Capitalism: A Response," *Discernment,* Winter 2001, p. 4.

[7]Sider, "Ethical Challenges," p. 3.

[8]Kenneth Chase, "Globalization & Christian Ethics," *Discernment,* Winter 2001, p. 1.

[9]Hervé Carrier, *Evangelizing the Culture of Modernity* (Maryknoll, N.Y.: Orbis, 1993), p. 2.

[10]Jim Wallis, *The Soul of Politics: A Practical and Prophetic Vision for Change* (New York: New Press/Orbis, 1994), 71.

[11]Václav Havel, quoted in Steven Erlanger, "Heed the Voices of the People," *New York Times,* August 23, 2000, late edition, sec. A, p. 8, col. 1.

[12]Len Doyal and Ian Gough, *Theory of Human Need* (New York: Guilford, 1991), p. 11.

[13]Robert Chambers, *Poverty in India: Concepts, Research and Reality* (Brighton, England: Institute of Development Studies, 1988), p. 18.

[14]Jayakumar Christian, "An Alternate Reading of Poverty," in *Working with the Poor,* ed. Bryant Myers (Monrovia, Calif.: World Vision, 1999), p. 23.

Chapter 14: Global Engagement

[1]Hans Küng, *Global Responsibility: In Search of a New World Ethic* (New York: Crossroad, 1991), p. 136.

[2]Sarah Lyall, "In Nobel Talk, Annan Sees Each Human Life as the Prize," *New York Times,* December 11, 2001, late edition, sec. A, p. 3, col. 1.

[3]David Crane, "Giving More to Poor Essential, Leaders Told," *Toronto Star,* February 3, 2002.

[4]Ibid.

[5]Brian D. McLaren, *A New Kind of Christian: A Tale of Two Friends on a Spiritual Journey* (San Francisco: Jossey-Bass, 2001), pp. 112-13.

[6]John Gray, "Where There Is No Common Power," *Harper's,* December 2001, p. 15.

[7]The aid that is sent to Colombia is primarily intended to discourage the drug trade and generate alternative crops which in turn will hopefully curtail the export of drugs to America.

[8]John Paul II, address posted on CNN.com, December 25, 2001.

[9]Bryant L. Myers, *Walking with the Poor: Principles and Practices of Transformational Development* (Maryknoll, N.Y.: Orbis, 1999), p. 3.

[10]Craig R. Whitney, "The World: Hands Off; The No Mans Land in the Fight for Human Right," *New York Times,* December 12, 1999, p. 1, col. 1.

[11]Ron Sider, "The Ethical Challenges of Global Capitalism," *Discernment,* Winter 2001, p. 3.

[12]Andrew Walls, professor emeritus, University of Edinburgh, quoted by Andrew Walls, "Eusebius Tries Again: Reconceiving the Study of Christian History," *International Bulletin of Missionary Research,* July 2000, pp. 105-11.

[13]Samuel Escobar, "The Global Scenario at the Turn of the Century," in *Global Missiology for the Twenty-first Century: The Iguassu Dialogue,* ed. William D. Taylor (Grand Rapids, Mich.: Baker Academic, 2000), p. 28.

[14]Ibid.

[15]John Howard Yoder, *The Politics of Jesus* (Carlisle, U.K.: Paternoster, 1994), pp. 154-55.

[16]Küng, *Global Responsibility,* p. 46.

[17]Myers, *Walking with the Poor,* p. 57.

[18]Jayakumar Christian, "An Alternate Reading of Poverty," in *Working with the Poor,* ed. Bryant Myers (Monrovia, Calif.: World Vision, 1999), p. 3.

[19]Myers, *Walking with the Poor,* p. 13.

[20]Jim Wallis, *The Soul of Politics: A Practical and Prophetic Vision for Change* (New York: New Press, 1994), p. 151.

Chapter 15: Self Care: Nurturing a Mature Spine of Identity

[1]Peter Berger, quoted by David E. Wells, *God in the Wasteland* (Grand Rapids, Mich.: Eerdmans, 1994), p. 3.

[2]Gerard Kelly, *Retrofuture: Rediscovering Our Roots, Recharting Our Routes* (Downers Grove, Ill.: InterVarsity Press, 1999), p. 121.

[3]Paul Vitz, *Mars Hill* audiotape, July/August 1994, side 1.

[4]Eugene Peterson, *Earth and Altar*, quoted in "Reflections: Classic and Contemporary Excerpts on Beauty, Prayer, and Loving God," *Christianity Today*, July 10, 2000, p. 45.

[5]Myron and Jan Chartier, "Clergy Self-Care," *Clergy Journal*, p. 3.

[6]Michael Adams, *Sex in the Snow: Canadian Social Values at the End of the Millennium* (Toronto: Penguin, 1997), pp. 9-10.

[7]Simone Weil, quoted in "Quotations on the Many Views of Wisdom," *Living Pulpit*, July/September 2000, p. 32.

[8]Robert Wuthnow, *After Heaven: Spirituality in America Since the 1950s* (Berkeley: University of California Press, 1998), p. 14.

Chapter 16: Soul Care: Scripting My Story in God's Story

[1]Michael Riddell, *Threshold of the Future: Reforming the Church in the Post-Christian West* (London: SPCK, 1998), p. 12.

[2]Eugene Kennedy, quoted by Martin Marty, "Spiritual Junk Food Abounds," *Context*, January 1, 1999 (From the New World, August 30-September 6, 1998), p. 2.

[3]Miss Manners, quoted in *Propositions* (Institute for American Values), Summer 2000.

[4]Michael Adams, *Sex in the Snow: Canadian Social Values at the End of the Millennium* (Toronto: Penguin), p. 20.

[5]Gerard Kelly, *Retrofuture: Rediscovering Our Roots, Recharting Our Routes* (Downers Grove, Ill.: InterVarsity Press, 1999), pp. 131-32.

[6]C. Kirk Hadaway and David A. Roozen, *Rerouting the Protestant Mainstream: Sources of Growth and Opportunities for Change* (Nashville: Abingdon, 1995), p. 83.

[7]Marva J. Dawn, *A Royal "Waste" of Time: The Splendor of Worshiping God and Being Church for the World* (Grand Rapids, Mich.: Eerdmans, 1999), p. 1.

[8]See Richard J. Foster, *Streams of Living Water: Celebrating the Great Traditions of Christian Faith* (San Francisco: HarperSanFrancisco, 1998).

[9]Thomas Merton, *Thoughts in Solitude*, quoted in Martin Marty, "Saints Are Spirits Trying to Be Human," *Context*, May 15, 2000, p. 1.

[10]Joan Chittister, *Illuminated Life: Monastic Wisdom for Seekers of Light* (Maryknoll, N.Y.: Orbis, 2000), p. 107.

Chapter 17: Outreach: Making Meaning of God's Gospel Story

[1]Gerard Kelly, *Retrofuture: Rediscovering Our Roots, Recharting Our Routes* (Downers Grove, Ill.: InterVarsity Press, 1999), p. 209.

[2]Anthony Pappas and Scott Planting, *Mission: The Small Church Reaches Out* (Valley Forge, Penn.: Judson, 1993), p. xii.

[3]Gabriel Moran, *Showing How: The Act of Teaching* (Valley Forge, Penn.: Trinity Press International, 1997), p. 54.

[4]Walter Brueggemann, "The Legitimacy of a Sectarian Hermeneutic: 2 Kings 18-19," in *Education for Citizenship and Discipleship*, ed. Mary C. Boys (New York: Pilgrim, 1989), p. 6.

[5]John Drane, *Evangelism for a New Age: Creating Churches for the Next Century* (London: Marshall Pickering, 1994), p. 15.

[6]Os Guinness, *Fit Bodies, Fat Minds* (London: Hodder & Stoughton, 1994), p. 105.

[7]Richard Longenecker, *New Wine into Fresh Wineskins* (Peabody, Mass.: Hendrickson, 1999), p. 2.

[8]David Bosch, *Transforming Mission* (Maryknoll, N.Y.: Orbis, 1991), p. 353.

[9]Leonard Sweet, *Soul Tsunami: Sink or Swim in New Millennium Culture* (Grand Rapids, Mich.: Zondervan, 1999), p. 425.

[10]Frederick Buechner, *Wishful Thinking: A Theological ABC* (New York: Harper & Row, 1973), p. 32.

Chapter 18: Social Care: Pursuing God's Justice Story

[1]Roger Kimball, "Tenured Radicals," *New Criterion*, January 1991, p. 13.

[2]Robert E. Logan and Larry Short, *Mobilizing for Compassion: Moving People into Ministry* (Grand Rapids, Mich.: Fleming H. Revell, 1994), p. 11.

[3]Francis A. Schaeffer, *The Church at the End of the Twenty-first Century* (London: Norfolk, 1970), p. 51.

[4]Bishop Robinson Cavalcanti, address presented in Brazil, December 1999.

[5]Jacques Ellul, *The Presence of the Kingdom* (Colorado Springs, Colo.: Helmers and Howard, 1989), p. 35.

[6]Dorothy Bloom, *Church Doors Open Outward* (Valley Forge, Penn.: Judson, 1987), p. 15.

[7]Craig van Gelder, quoted in Darrell L. Guder et al., eds., *Missional Church: A Vision for the Sending of the Church in North America* (Grand Rapids, Mich.: Eerdmans, 1998), p. 54.

[8]Anita Roddick, *Business as Unusual* (London: Thorsons, 2000).

[9]Don E. Eberly, *Restoring the Good Society* (Grand Rapids, Mich.: Baker, 1994), p. 16.

[10]Richard J. Mouw, *Uncommon Decency: Christian Civility in an Uncivil World* (Downers Grove, Ill.: InterVarsity Press, 1992), p. 20.

[11]Nicholas Wolterstorff, "The Contours of Justice: An Ancient Call for Shalom," in *God and the Victim*, ed. Lisa Barnes Lampman (Grand Rapids, Mich.: Eerdmans, 1999).